Life by a
Thousand Cuts

For Mom and Dad

No life is meaningful unless shared.

— David Crump

Acknowledgments

This book is made possible because of the generous love and support of family, friends, colleagues and the medical providers I have been blessed to have as a part of my life's journey thus far. No acknowledgment would be complete without thanks and appreciation to each of them individually and I do that below.

First and foremost, thank you Mom and Dad! You gave me the gift of life; nurtured, developed, loved unconditionally, scolded me and shared my triumphs and failures; became exasperated at times; expressed pride; laughed and cried with me and otherwise proved me to be one of life's winners in the genetic lottery. No kid could ask for better!

Melissa and Michael Cook and Susan and David Hammond, thank you for being the wonderful sisters and brothers-in-law that you are. I am grateful for you!

Thank you to the "LFP Neighbors" (David and Tracey Lyman and Bob (PMA Baby!) and Elizabeth Wolfe) for being there with and for me during the toughest times in both the cancer battle and the divorce process. You shared and cared, encouraged survival, put food out for me and brought laughter, humor and a much needed sense of normalcy and hope. In the worst times I never felt more loved or loving.

My second family, John Budlong, Starla Hohbach, Debbie Watt, Tara Eubanks, Joe Cunnane, Lesleigh Rosen, Brian Leonard and Faye Wong made the office a place I wanted to come back to and made the coming back possible. The Budlong Law Firm fought a different kind of fight on my behalf that lasted well over three years. There are no finer or more courageous lawyers and they fear no battle.

Eric Fong, Bruce Lambrecht, Amy Goertz, Richard and Jo Ann Downs, Andy Bergh, Mary Ruth Mann, Jim Kytle, Mary Jo Oxrieder and Windwalker "Windy" Taibi are colleagues and friends I have been privileged to know and work with. In the end, what we take from life are the relationships and yours are cherished.

James "Jim" Moriarty, thank you for inspiring me to focus on "goodness".

Warren Buffett and Charlie Munger will never know my name but I thank them for their published wit, wisdom and sage advice that has me saved costly mistakes and helped me focus on swinging only at the fat pitches.

Robert Cialdini, Clotaire Rapaille, Tim Galwey, David Foster Wallace (1962-2008), Christopher Hitchens (1949-2011), Bill Bryson and Nassim N. Taleb likewise will never know my name but each of them are giants and "King Hell" thinkers. Their books have provided me with hours and hours of thought-provoking insights.

Paul Luvera and Gerry Spence (and the Spence Trial Lawyers College in Dubois, Wyoming) are the very best at what they do – lawyering for people – and are the standards of excellence, as measured by results, by which I measure professional success, emulate and strive to be like each and every day. Thank you Paul Luvera for giving me a seat at the PALS' table and for teaching me about "paper tigers" and "trials as battles of perception". Thank you Gerry Spence for making possible for me the privilege of being a Warrior, for teaching me to "live an artistic life", to "flow with the river" and to "just be real". Thank you also David Ball for showing me how to make a great opening statement and Rick

Friedman for *"Rules of the Road"* and *"Polarizing the Case"*.

J.L. Moreno, M.D. (1889-1974) (through his written works), Don Clarkson, M.S.W., Kathie St. Clair, M.S.W., John Nolte, Ph.D. and Katlin Larimer, M.S.W. helped teach and show me how to artfully direct others and appreciate how to use the tools of psychodramatic reenactment and sociometry for personal and professional growth.

O.R. "Rhody" Elofson, Ph.D. is a good friend and mentor and we have shared countless written and face-to-face exchanges about all manner of things. Rhody makes a bold cup of coffee and the best Manhattan around and listens patiently as I ponder the big questions of life and their answers. I am hoping that one of these days he will confirm that indeed, I have at last solved them.

John Gottman, Ph.D., through his weekend workshop for couples at The Gottman Institute, taught me the invaluable lesson that even good people with the best of intentions can fall into unsustainable and unhealthy relationships and that compatibility is the key to lasting love.

Susan Selby is a singular gem of a person. Susan may not be a medical doctor, but I'm convinced she knows more about medicine than some of them. Susan was there, every step of the way, in the darkest moments even as she shouldered and managed her own and others' significant burdens, and always found a way to put a hopeful perspective on the situation.

William G. Friend, M.D. developed the ColoCare© test and has saved countless lives. He fearlessly and authentically put himself and his reputation on the line for me and helped put a warm, passionate human face on what might otherwise have been a meaningless statistic. I am convinced he was our "Lightning in a

Bottle" that made every difference.

Rick Carrithers is, among other things, a fellow-survivor who would have "killed for (my) number". Rick hired me fresh out of law school and impressed on me the need to "marry the facts" and "avoid fuzzy thinking". Rick learned from the best at Yale and taught me that if you can't explain it to someone simply then you simply don't understand what you're talking about. Rick also introduced me, when I was at my worst, to the trout-filled Basin Lakes of Eastern Washington and urged me to appreciate the roadside geology, the Missoula Flood, and the world of subsurface fly fishing (the edges, hedges and ledges). Rick generously shared his expertly hand-tied nymphs and strike indicators and taught me the "system", even as he decried me the "moocher" that I was. Rick also gave me a dedicated professional purpose in a tough time and proved to be supremely generous when he didn't have to be. I am forever grateful.

Jamie Gobel is a bright shining light of a genuine person that I met near the end of chemotherapy. Our medical diagnoses were similar but Jamie's path has been longer. Jamie is my Hero!

John, Paul, George and Ringo provide the soundtrack for many days and nights and showed me that the path to creative genius can be littered with cacophonous noise.

Keith and Giuli Johnston, David and Molly Roth, Ron and Debbie Plunkett and Lance and Julie Rexroat are lifelong friends. We've climbed mountains together, sailed, biked, hiked, skied, hunted, fished, camped, laughed, traveled, rolled our eyes, had too much to drink and otherwise provided reliable witness to one another's lives.

Cliff Hollenbeck provided much appreciated and helpful advice about book publishing and gave lift to the wings of this project that lay idle far too long.

Natalie Chantal Luke is my partner and my love. No one is more generous and caring. In the words of The Beatles: "She gives me everything, and tenderly." Natalie has created a nurturing, positive environment that helps me thrive and be everything I can be, both personally and professionally.

Thank you each and every individual who first read these essays on WordPress and provided insightful comments and feedback.

Last but certainly and by no means least, thank you to the physicians, surgeons, specialists, nurses, technicians, staff and the countless thousands of dedicated research scientists devoting their lives to early detection, to finding a cure for cancer and giving second chances, hope and quality of life to deserving people everywhere. Thank you Dr. Little, Dr. MacFarlane and Dr. Ward – my team of experts.

Contents

Introduction

This book is the result of a flash of inspiration and a little bit of earnest follow-through. After two difficult years, where my health had been a serious issue, I found myself one Saturday morning in late-November 2009 gazing at the ever-luminous screen of my Dell laptop and thinking that I had something to say but not having anyone around to say it to. That I had been through a lot in those two years, it seemed, could provide some interesting reflections and observations, if only, in the end, for me, and via the process that might help make sense of what, I came to find, could not really be made sense of. This is not better illustrated, for me, than by the well-meaning intones along the lines of "Well, you know, things happen for a reason". Do they? I thought not. But I did and still do believe that a person can find real "meaning" in things that happen, if that person is open to finding it. For me, finding that meaning was a task made easier by putting pen to paper (or in this case digits to keypad). So knowing full well that I was likely to drop the project like a hot potato along the way, and sooner than later at that, I opened a free blog account at WordPress. Now understand, I had read, perhaps, a half-dozen blogs to that point, usually by accident if a Google search pointed me there. In fact, to this day, I have little interest in reading the blogs of others. So I readily accepted that I should forgive any and all who never cared to read mine, and even more so, greatly appreciated everyone who cared to read what I had written.

I often remind myself that it's helpful to know where I'm going before starting out. In this instance, I didn't know where I was going. All I had was a faint notion that I'd make one blog entry per week, every Saturday morning, for a year.

I also knew that, for me, an important part of the creative process would be receiving feedback. It seemed that I could gain some understandings, both through the process of writing, and in reading the comments and responses. At the same time, I also believed it was important to honor the feedback by allowing the comments and responses to rest as the final say. In other words, I made it a point to not respond in kind, but rather to encourage any and all feedback without fear of chill or reprisal. I didn't want to engage in debate, only encourage it among others, then sit back and enjoy the conversations from afar.

As it turned out, other than for a time in the noble beginning, I didn't manage to adhere to the "one entry per week" mandate. But, in the end, I was able to average an entry every other week. And that seemed about right by the time November 2010 rolled around. I'd enjoyed the process, learned to see some things in new and perhaps better ways, revised my personal history, received helpful feedback, encouraged a bit of conversation, made new friends, and been reminded of my own aptitudes, accomplishments, weaknesses and failures. I still enjoy reading these essays and I hope you, the reader, can learn or feel something meaningful as well.

A New Frontier

Seems every day we're presented with new opportunities and new challenges that in and of themselves present opportunities. I call it being open to the possibilities, or occasionally utter the phrase "expand your universe of opportunities". Well, today is Blog Day One and I have to share that I'm kind of excited about this new tool. I believe that more than ever before I may have something valuable to say. I've certainly gained some perspective from experience that I didn't have 22 months ago, and future Blog posts will touch on some of that experience. I invite any and all to share in return. I also intend to use this forum for thoughts and exchanges about aspects of being a trial lawyer, and about career and health issues in general. We all have a lot to learn from one another. Let's let the learning begin.

The Decade From Hell

There's a particularly well-written and readable article in Time magazine this week that I just happened to see online this morning. The gist is that the 2000's were, in many ways, the worst decade since, well, anyone can really remember, at least for our nation. We all witnessed the "bookends" of 9/11 and the Great Recession, and everything in between (Katrina, Afghanistan). We find ourselves worse off economically than this time 10 years ago. Unemployment exceeds 10% and home values have fallen precipitously. We feel less safe on our own shores. Our nation's infrastructure is in decline. But all is not lost, and there is great promise ahead, a "reversion to the mean" to quote the author. And that's what struck me most, the notion that things will get better. Decades somehow seem to develop a character all their own. Time has anointed the 2000's as the Decade from Hell. That describes my personal experience too. Let us hope that the 2010's will be at worst a regression to the (good old) mean and at best a time of sustained peace, economic prosperity, security and grace.

Life Lessons

If I had a son or daughter I would like them to do well in life. While scholarly instruction is a time-tested means of teaching and learning information, I've come to believe that there is no substitute for real-life experience, i.e. action and self-discovery. But action and self-discovery need to be tempered with good judgment. With that in mind, when my child reached a certain age of understanding, I would like to make a gift of ten books that I believe would help develop skills and understandings that years of traditional curriculum might likely fail to deliver.

These books touch on fundamental life concepts of action, empathy, being genuine, decision-making, communication, persuasion, rapport, and avoiding mistakes. In no particular order, here they are, with room for one to make a rounded ten:

The Snowball – Warren Buffett and the Business of Life by Alice Schroeder;

Influence: The Psychology of Persuasion and *Influence: Science and Practice*, both by Robert Cialdini, PhD;

The Selfish Gene by Richard Dawkins;

Acting In by Adam Blatner, MD;

Emotional Intelligence and Social Intelligence, both by Daniel Goleman;

How to Win Friends and Influence People by Dale Carnegie;

The Inner Game of Tennis by W. Timothy Gallwey.

There are no books here on spiritual matters. That's because the subject is huge and hugely personal. I'd want my child to make those discoveries for him or herself. Still, if there is something you recommend to fill that tenth spot then please share. Also, please feel free to comment and suggest any of your own favorites on any topic, fiction or non-fiction.

Thank You Jim

Last week a friend sent a private email in response to the post, Life Lessons, and the blog tag line "Seeking to achieve greatness".

He said:

"(David), Greatness is a great aspiration – but a lot of people should just focus on Goodness. Much more attainable, and does not require as much external validation."

Well, that caught my attention. It inspired me to question my goals and, perhaps more important, the motivations behind those goals. Can a large part of those motivations be, as my friend suggests, the insatiable craving (my words) for external validation? And if so, then what? Would the critical ego-self that resides within even recognize greatness if it were achieved? I'm guessing not, such being the nature of the critical ego-self. (For more on this read *The*

Inner Game of Tennis by W. Timothy Gallwey.)

So thank you Jim. Henceforth the tag on this humble blog will read "Seeking to achieve goodness". I'm hoping this revised aspiration will help point to a good life that is every bit as meaningful as a great one, and without all the extra pressures.

Finally, thanks also to everyone who posted publicly or privately with their book recommendations. You are appreciated. Here are two more that were recommended by folks too shy to post: 1) *The Power of Now* by Eckhart Tolle; and 2) *Hope for the Flowers* by Trina Paulus.

Do A Stillpoint

I've been trying to come up with a meaningful topic for this week, without forcing the issue. Late one bedtime I picked out a small book of meditations, not for blog inspiration, just to add to my already crowded little night-stand. Opening the book to a random page I found this:

"Bringing awareness to our breathing, we remind ourselves that we are here now."

I don't breathe enough, often enough, deeply enough. I need to stand up and publicly shout that "Yes, I inhale, deeply and often". Here it is all around us, air, the most freely available resource on the planet, and yet I don't take my share. What a shame.

The author of my little book of meditations says:

"Breathing is home. It's where you can go when you're not sure what you need, when you don't know what else to do... You go home to breathing by focusing your attention to it... At any time, in any place, when you need to be calm, when you're upset, when you're distracted... focus on your breathing."

He calls this "doing a Stillpoint". You would think something so simple, so fundamental, so life-sustaining would be made easy by nature's grace. I'm finding otherwise. But I intend to keep practicing, and breathing.

What Is Your Satisfaction?

'Tis the season… to be jolly, of course… to connect and reconnect with family, friends, colleagues and loved ones, surely. There is no phenomenon in our culture quite like Christmas. I imagine each and every one of us can remember at some time in our lives the innocence of believing in Santa, and the eagerness and anticipation of his visit. And if we can't remember that for ourselves, certainly we can remember it through the eyes of our children.

'Tis also the season we grown-ups come, like Greeks, bearing gifts… the fruits of seemingly endless shopping, spending, wrapping, packing, traveling and mailing. I ponder, without being judgmental, the motivations behind holiday gifting. Do we give out of obligation, out of a desire for power and prestige, or out of genuine joy, grace and compassion? I am not suggesting our motivation has to be the exclusive domain and province of one or the other, only that, when shopping for gifts at Christmastime, who among us will deny keeping at least one eye open for our own self's material wants?

Maybe obligatory gifting is a good thing. After all, it has the potential at least for us to be thinking of, and doing for, others… to show and express our appreciation in a material way (as if words or actions alone are not enough). Maybe Holiday gifting is nothing more than another means of expression, of communicating our thoughts to, for and about another person. In that context then, it seems, it really is the thought that counts. So is it really better to give than to receive? I think it depends. Think of it this way; isn't a thoughtful, genuine communication more likely to be appreciated and well-received? And if a communication is obligatory (take, for example, "I love you" when that is not so), are we doing the recipient of the message (or gift) a favor? Maybe in that context it's better not to give.

Where is the joy for you in Christmas? What is your satisfaction, when so much of the Holiday is about material splendor; tangible things? I can't speak for anyone else, but I do know that a hug and a kind word, genuinely expressed, are worth more to me than any material gift (except, perhaps, the gifts of love and health, which really aren't material in the sense). However, if you insist, I'll forego the hug if you'll just leave the keys to the Bentley (or Prius) under the tree.

Auld Lang Syne

Auld Lang Syne
n. The times gone past; the good old days.

How many of you know the words to Auld Lang Syne, or that it was written by Scottish poet Robert Burns? This year I am printing it out, for myself and friends, and will sing it, for the first time, with understanding.

Should old acquaintance be forgot
And never brought to mind?
Should old acquaintance be forgot
And auld lang syne.

CHORUS:

For auld lang syne, my dear,
For auld lang syne,

We'll take a cup of kindness yet,
For auld lang syne.

And surely you'll buy your cup
And surely I'll buy mine.
And we'll take a cup o' kindness yet
For auld lang syne.

We two have run about the slopes
And picked the daisies fine.
But we've wandered many a weary foot
Since auld lang syne.

We two have paddled in the stream
From morning sun till dine.
But seas between us broad have roared
Since auld lang syne.

And there's a hand my trusty friend
And give us a hand o' thine.
And we'll take a right good-will draught,
For auld lang syne.

HAPPY NEW YEAR!

Saint Elizabeth

My friend and neighbor Elizabeth is doing something extraordinary in 3 weeks – she is donating a kidney to a friend of hers, a person in real need. I know a little bit about kidneys, having spent the better part of last year working on a medical negligence case that involved the needless loss of a kidney. This is no small contribution, and no minor inconvenience, considering the time and tests required to qualify as a donor, the risks of surgery, and the recovery experience. It's a huge gift. It makes me feel small, but also causes me to swell with pride knowing that I know Elizabeth. She is a true giving person. Last year she traveled to Africa for a month, at her own expense, to hold babies, teach classes to children, and generally help wherever help was needed. She makes a difference. Elizabeth is a nurturing person, and that can be attested to by her (and others') children, numerous small (and not so small) animals, her own family, friends, neighbors, the families that she nannies for, and the women that she assisted as a "doula" (a birthing coach). She gives life, helps life and now, saves life. I don't honestly know where the energy comes from. I think of the times I have tried to do good for others, and in one act of unselfish generosity she has outdone my life's work in that regard. I accept that we can't all be saints, but I have anointed her, my friend and neighbor, "Saint Elizabeth".

Cancer – Part 1

Exactly two years ago I had a diagnosis of cancer; stage 3B; operable, but with the need for immediate surgery, chemotherapy and radiation. Seven surgeries, nine hospitalizations, many CT and MRI scans, and countless office visits later, I feel grateful to be here now, writing this blog post. It's a world I don't wish on anyone. And yet now, after, and even when being in that world, there are things that can be taken from it – worthwhile things. It can be an eye-opener. It can challenge you to become more mature. It can clarify your fundamental values almost instantly. It can send you into a panic from which you learn to deal and cope. It can bring people closer to you, and bring you closer to them. It can be like a long forced march into the snow and mud of a Russian winter. It can teach you patience (whether you like it or not). It can teach you that you seldom remember pain, once it's behind you. It can open your eyes to the fact that anywhere you are, if you look left and then right, you are likely to see someone who is worse off than you. It can awaken you to the fact that there are hundreds and hundreds of people actually working to keep you alive. It can help you appreciate your life now. It can make you sad. It can make you angry and inspire you to become stronger. It can frustrate you and force you to overcome. It can open your mind to new spiritual directions. It can cause you to wake up in the middle of the night soaked through with sweat and shivering. It can put you in place to meet a lot of new and interesting people. It can put your life entirely in the hands of others and teach you to have faith and trust. It can teach you humility. It can teach you prayer. It can teach you that there is no modesty in a hospital. It can teach you that the fastest way to forget about your own predicament (albeit temporarily) is to show genuine interest in someone else. It can be helped if you keep a positive mental attitude. It can ruin a good night's sleep. It can help you lose 40 pounds faster than any diet. It can make a breakfast of Cream of Wheat taste as good as a steak. It can tire you out in the day. It will want you to ask "Why me?" You can refuse to ask that question! It will give you an opportunity to assess how much you really value your life and living it.

It will give others the opportunity to help you, and you the opportunity to let others help. It can give others the opportunity to reflect on how they really feel about you. It can reveal to you the amazing generosity and kindness of others. It will give you an opportunity to be a role model. It will reinforce the importance of early detection. I repeat, it will reinforce the importance of early detection. It will let you easily forget the hard times and discomfort once you feel good again. It can show you that some things you once worried about are the "small stuff" in the bigger picture. It can give you a glimpse of what it's like to walk in the Shadow of the Valley. It can cause you to crave ice cream. There are worse things. It can let you keep a sense of humor. It can teach you the power of a hug. It can teach, and you can learn, myriad lessons from it if you are open to looking for meanings. It can give you a second chance. So, to all my family, friends, colleagues, health-care providers and fellow travelers on that particular journey, "thank you".

SCUBA – Just Plain Fun

In these shorter and rainy days of winter, my thoughts turn to the warmer, sunnier climes of Hawaii, the Caribbean, Mexico, and the gentle oceans that are home to my "alien" friends: the innumerable big and small fish, the moray eels, sharks, stingrays, Manta rays, octopus, crabs, shrimp, lobsters, dolphins, barracuda, turtles, sea lions, and the coral and shipwrecks they all swim through and around. It's been over 4 years since my last dives, and I miss it terribly. There was a time when taking two dive vacations a year was the norm. Why do I like diving so much? Well, for one thing, it's as close to a feeling of weightlessness as you can get here on Earth (with the exception of NASA's "vomit comet", and that isn't exactly "Earthly" in its parabolic flight). For another, it's relaxing and meditative. Tropical waters envelope your body like a second skin. Your breathing is measured and relaxed.

You hear each breath too, in and out. (Think Darth Vader.) It's meditative. Your movements are subtle and you can glide and soar like an acrobat in slow motion. When you think about it, you are, literally, flying. There are times when I have drifted along in a strong current for a mile or more, upside down, vertical, just for the fun of it, looking out at the undersea world from that unusual perspective. Try doing that on land. There are times when I just sit myself down on the ocean floor and look all around me, never knowing what I might see gliding by, or hiding from me, hoping to not be eaten. Other times I am curious, peering into every cave and cranny, never knowing what I might find looking back out at me with big or small eyes. Sometimes what's there has big, sharp teeth. It's a rare privilege and opportunity to visit this "alien" world.

Undersea creatures are Earthly but they might just as well be from another planet, or more accurately, since we humans are the visitors, we're the ones from another planet. As far as I'm concerned, when I scuba dive I am just a respectful visitor to another world. Also, the equipment is getting better, safer and easier to use every day. And scuba is a buddy activity, so in that way, it's a sharing opportunity. It's meaningful in the sense that an experience shared with another person can be more memorable. You never really know what you'll come across at 5 to 7 fathoms (30 to 42 feet) or anywhere on or below the ocean's surface. Now and then you get a surprise of your life. A giant Manta glides by, curious, then makes a big arc, returns, and tips its wings in respectful salute; or a pod of wild dolphins happens along and you hurry to jump in, swimming with them for a time, entranced by their sweet dolphin smiles, but knowing from their eyes that they are wary of this glass-eyed creature with big feet who wants to play. And divers as a group seem to be good-natured people. I have made lifelong friends on these trips. It's also a great way to lower your core temperature early in the day in a hot climate, and work up a hearty appetite for lunch, before taking in some poolside or beach-side action for the afternoon. It's an activity that's easy to learn, not terribly expensive, and accessible for people of all ages. I had a chronic bad back for some years, and the feeling of weightlessness (neutral buoyancy) relieved the spinal compression and let me get swimming exercise without discomfort. In the end, it's also a journey back to the primordial soup (the womb?) whence we might possibly have emerged from. Call it a homecoming, of sorts. Call it a Baptism. Or call it a cleansing every time you jump in. Heck, just call it FUN.

Second Chances
(If Only I Knew Then)

Lately I have been having a time of my life, thanks to Facebook, and the really great friends and individuals that I've been privileged to reconnect with after so many years. Some of them I never expected to encounter ever again. Some of them, I am learning, thought of me as a friend, or sweetly, and I didn't really know it at the time. Now there's a real gift; a new old friend. There seems to be an explosion of that kind of connection lately. And it feels good. How many of us have said, "If only I knew then what I know now"? I have said that, many times.

I attended a private co-ed boarding school in Central Florida, Howey Academy, in 1974. I was in 9th grade that year. My memories of freshman year are mixed; some good, some not so good. But it was 9th grade, after all. Who among us mortals had it so fortunate as to be at the top of the social, academic or athletic heap at 14 or 15?

Looking back over the yearbook, I'm reminded of how geographically diverse the student body was, and how remote the school was too, situated next to Little Lake Harris and nestled in among the gentle hills and nearby orange groves of the small town of Howey in the Hills. Blink and you missed it. Forty miles from Orlando, we had 271 students that year, grades 7-12, and they came from places nearby (Florida, of course, and Georgia), and as far away as Brazil, Peru, Honduras, Ecuador, Venezuela, South Africa, Aruba, El Salvador, Antigua, the Bahamas, Dominica (British West Indies), Quebec, New Jersey, Michigan, Maine, Illinois, South Carolina, Alabama, New York, New Hampshire, Washington, D.C., Ohio, Mississippi, California, Illinois, Louisiana, Puerto Rico, Tortola (British Virgin Islands), and Jamaica. We even had one kid from Neptune (well, Neptune Beach, Florida, but still). I'm truly astounded looking back at how far-ranging the student body was for that small number of us. We even had two sets of twins, as I remember. Unfortunately, I do not recall there being a single black classmate.

I do recall struggling to find my place there, and feeling out of it (my place, that is). The older kids, especially the seniors, all seemed like full-fledged adults. At least they looked a lot older. Even now, when I scan the annual from that year, I still see those faces as I did back then. I still feel the same rumble of adolescent, pubescent and young-adult emotions that I carried around inside of me then; and I do mean inside of me, struggling to find a way out, to be communicated, and shared. That's part of the reason why I am writing this. You see, I have been experiencing the privilege of getting to know then what I know now. In these reconnections I am feeling more fully human, more able to communicate meaningfully, more genuine, more caring, interested and evolved. I find that I am saying many, if not all of those things that I so very much wanted to say back then, but, for whatever reasons, either did not, could not, or would not. I feel transported back to that time and place, and I find that I'm still the same person, only I feel more interesting and more interested. I'm seeing things with new eyes, a whole heart and a deeper spirit.

But most of all, I love the feeling and power (benevolent power, "awareness" if you will) of being real; of being able to recognize what I feel; to acknowledge my feelings as valid; and to share them in a meaningful way, at long last, with individuals that did not get the benefit then of the "full David". (Unfortunately too many of them did get to experience a full of himself David.) I seemed to have little comfort or facility with the language of feelings in 1974 (and a lot of years after that, truth be told). And guess what? I wasn't alone. What is interesting though is how each and every person I've reconnected with from Howey Academy (then Florida's largest co-ed boarding school) had a different experience. Some say they loved it, were truly happy there, and felt a sense of being free and in charge of their own lives for the first time. Others were troubled by turbulent current events. Some simply shined, gloriously. Others, like me, were figuring it all out, or trying to; just moving forward and hoping, believing, things would one day come together. Here's how my roommate, a good person, a smart person, saw me back then, from the words he forever penned into my yearbook: "Dave... You've got a lot of enthusiasm for life which is good and no control over it, which is bad. Learn serenity and you'll go far. You'd better, 'cause if you don't, you're gonna get thrown in jail". Well, I'm still trying to learn serenity (why wasn't it offered as an elective?) but so far have managed to avoid jail. (In full disclosure, I did spend one anxious night in the Whitman County Jail in 1979, but that was college, another time, and another story.) Some of you know that I developed a passion for learning about psychodrama. Psychodrama, as I studied it, is an "action method" developed by J.L. Moreno for discovering the truth, and for the dual purposes of learning new and more appropriate responses to old, recurring situations; and healthy, spontaneous and appropriate responses to new situations. In psychodrama there's a saying: "Every experience should be experienced twice". I take that to mean that the first time, if needed or desired, can be a practice run while the second time can be an opportunity to apply the lessons we have learned, and hopefully allow us to respond more appropriately. Let's call it a "second chance". Well that's what I've been having a lot of lately, second chances, to show some of the world something more of parts of me that weren't so accessible then, and to learn more about parts of others that are special and well worth the investment of time and effort to seek and find. So thank you Facebook. Keep up the good work. You've brought me more than a few smiles, and some new and old memories in a very short time. And just think, I still have eleven more grades to explore (fifteen if you count college; eighteen counting law school).

Why I Love The Beatles

I love The Beatles. John, Paul, George and Ringo are synonymous with great music, rock and roll culture, youth, peace, and love. They arrived on the scene, fresh-faced. They grew as we (the culture of the '60's) grew. They broke up, sadly, at the dawn of a new decade. The Beatles were the '60's, from the first "One, two, three, foh!" as Paul sings urgently that "she was just 17" when he saw her "standing there", looking "way beyond compare", to the dissonant climactic orchestral and piano finale of Sergeant Pepper's A Day in the Life, to the medley from Abbey Road ("And in the end, the love you take, is equal to the love, you make"); all that, and everything in between, accomplished in a mere 8 years.

Every Beatles fan has his or her favorite Beatle, Beatles songs, albums and probably even eras. In my unscientific way, I've determined there are three distinct Beatle eras, though I can easily be persuaded that the number is four (okay, maybe five). I wonder if any psychology graduate student ever attempted to correlate personality traits from standardized personality inventories with Beatles' songs, albums or eras. It would be an interesting study.

The first era has to begin with Please Please Me (recorded in only 12 hours). Here are the youthful innocents (not really so innocent according to biographers, as they had spent time playing long nights in Hamburg's Reeperbahn, the red light district). Conclude that first era, perhaps, with Hard Day's Night. The middle era reveals the lads from Liverpool becoming more confident and assertive, more experimental and more studio-savvy with Rubber Soul and Revolver. The middle era culminates magnificently with Sergeant Pepper's Lonely Hearts Club Band (the greatest record of all time according to Rolling Stone magazine). Then, for me anyway, things really get interesting. I think of the third era as the holy trinity: The White Album, Let It Be and Abbey Road. Now the band are growing up, are in their late 20's, and, sadly, are dealing with the weightier emotions borne of grown up experiences, like the death of their manager, deaths of family, friends and peers, mismanagement at Apple Corp., money problems, drug problems, rivalries, jealousies, distractions, new loves (Linda, Patti and Yoko) and ultimately, breaking up.

5 or 6 years ago, through the wonder of the Internet, I found a website where I could download (apparently legally, and for a small charge) hours and hours of unreleased Beatles outtakes, demos, and studio bits. The beautiful result ... they sound terrible; just awful; beyond awful; awful "way beyond compare". And I love that! I love that the band, THAT band, can sound like a parade of braying donkeys; like a carnival of angry cats. What I take from

these dissonant, discordant, disharmonious gems is the insight that making amazing music for posterity is a process, and that any creative endeavor must also be a process. Almost no one gets it right the first time. And it all starts with an idea, or sometimes it just starts with a start; a kernel, a rough nugget, shaped, polished, filtered, looped, dubbed, overlaid, played backward, sped up, or slowed down.

Without question The Beatles were individually, and as a group, great musicians, singers and songwriters. They had a magical chemistry and unparalleled charisma. They came along at a time when the perfect storm of television and mass communication to a worldwide audience was burgeoning. They came at a time when their message of peace and love resonated with a mass audience and was needed. They also had classically trained George Martin to produce their records, and the deep pocket resources of EMI (their recording company). But they had more than that. They also had certain "experiences" that shaped their creative ideas and output; letting them see things from very different perspectives. I'm talking about drugs, of course; pot, LSD, and reportedly more (for John). I'm convinced their well-documented experimentation was in pursuit of art and craft, and not the nihilistic tune in, turn on and drop out escapism advocated by Timothy Leary. I'm convinced that drug experimentation for The Beatles was about innovation, not about making a radical counter-cultural statement. I don't believe they were all that radical or counter-cultural. Their message was always peace and love, through words and music. I do believe they experimented, with drugs and other things, because they sought to have experiences that might lead them to make their music creatively different, if not downright great.

They were innovators, almost always original, and never derivative, as was true of many other bands of the time. They managed to avoid being categorized, catalogued and pigeon-holed. I think that's one reason why they endure. So often they made a record and made it their own by taking advantage of whatever happened to be available to them, using any and all resources creatively; unique instruments in unique ways; sound clips of animals, traffic, and laughter. Sure, now, looking back, we can say it's easy and that anyone can take bits, pieces and fragments of tape, cut them up, throw them in the air, let them fall to the floor, and then reassemble the pieces at random, or play songs or bits backward or faster or slower. But the fact is, they thought of it, they did it first, and they risked themselves doing it. I think there is a lot to be learned about that; about being creative; about taking chances. "Well, just jump in" my good friend once told me, and "Flow with the river" another said. You never quite know where the river will take you. This realization has freed me to take creative chances and in so doing to quiet the noise of the ego critic that lives within.

I like to paint in my garage in the summer when the days are sunny and warm. I like the door open and the natural light of a long summer day streaming in. I almost never start out with much, if anything, in the way of a concept. How can I? I have no formal art training of any kind. But I have learned, when painting, to take the pressure from myself and just jump in, giving myself permission to throw, slap, drip, dash and brush paint (or glue, or caulk, or putty, or tape or whatever) onto a canvas, this way and that, in odd assortments of colors and textures, brushing in what must seem like random (and maybe occasionally inspired) ways without the filter of critical thought. I challenge myself to be spontaneous, to act before my conscious mind is able to judge my actions and put on the brakes. And I keep working at it, sometimes over-working the canvas and ruining the thing, but that's okay. The point is, I am painting. And if there should be something of a finished product that surprises, delights or moves me, or someone else, then that is a welcome result. Almost invariably, there is a welcome result. And if I look at the finished painting long enough, deeply enough, all the different ways, rotating the canvas on one side after another, again and again and again, then, if I am open to the possibilities, I will see something amazing, something magical appear that wasn't evident at first glance. I don't know how or why this is so, but I do know I am not the only one this happens to. On more than one occasion I have introduced a friend to painting, out there in the garage, and watched with pleasure as he or she, who never painted before, created something valuable and meaningful. I think that's a good lesson. Anyone, with a little bit of inspiration, and the courage to jump in, can create something worthwhile.

So, "in the end", I love The Beatles because, when no one was listening, they could sound terrible. That tells me they are, after all, only human, just like the rest of us, and that inspires me.

Incompatibility
(Reflections of A Failed Marriage)

I was married for ten years, and divorced nearly five years ago. I've had a lot of time to think about the successes and mostly failures I experienced being married. I admit I failed as a husband. And when I think about it, in a sense, I failed in all of my romantic relationships. The proof is the simple fact that, at 51, I'm single, and still alone.

I've asked myself what kind of man enters into a loving relationship with a reasonably decent person, with his eyes and ears open, alert to his full senses, with every opportunity to learn as much about the other person as is probably needed, who takes a vow for better or worse, experiences moments of tenderness, and then gives up on it, a decade later, ruining a life together?

Well, having worked hard to identify the issues, and to gain insight into the behaviors and coping strategies that derailed my marriage, I may have found a few answers.

I can recall that early on, well before getting married, and even before getting engaged, there were instances where the couple that I was a part of seemed unable or unwilling to find even some measure of resolution in conflict. I recall that we did not see eye-to-eye or agree very often on things of importance, or even on insignificant things. And I also recall that we shared very little in the way of meaningful conversation. The best way I can describe the overall feeling of the relationship for me is that we were like two trains, chugging along on our own tracks, parallel, but rarely intersecting in a meaningful way for very long. To me, it seemed, we were too often on a journey without a common destination. I also recall thinking that we were probably not, nor ever likely to be, that couple that others looked at and wished they could be.

I want to make it clear that my purpose is not to assign blame or fault, or to air laundry or be judgmental. Instead, it's about acknowledging responsibility for my own actions and failings, and sharing a bit about what I learned along the way that will, hopefully, allow me to avoid repeating history.

From the beginning there were issues, differences and disagreements. Every couple has conflict. But, around the five-year mark, I began to very seriously question whether this marriage would, or should, survive. I sought answers from family, friends, peers and colleagues. That was unfair of me, asking others, indirectly, to tell me what to do. I'm sorry for putting them through that and I appreciate their patience, guidance and understanding. They know who they are.

I also read books on relationships and eventually sought help from a qualified professional. Even when I asked him the question, without ambiguity, the qualified professional would not give me the answer. This was not going to be easy, and full responsibility for the decision would have to be mine, alone.

He pointed out that I was "sublimating", putting most of my energies and passions into creative and recreational pursuits, professional groups, self-study, and my career. I had been telling myself that all of this inspired creativity, learning and redirected energy was healthy because it helped me to grow as a person, and was reassured that yes, to some degree, sublimation is healthy, but in my case was likely an indication that I was channeling energies outside of the relationship because I wasn't getting what I needed or wanted within it.

He helped me realize that I entered into the relationship with blinders on, and ignored the relational red flags that were there to be seen. Indeed, I am now convinced the red flags were visible and waving on the very first day.

But I was growing as a person, meeting new challenges, sharing with nurturing friends and peers, becoming more honest with myself, more willing to confront myself and others with the difficult questions and hard truths. I was transforming. But at home, or in the car together, or at dinner or in any room of the house, I felt alone and isolated; more so than I had ever felt before or since.

It was an agonizing five-year process before I finally faced the fear, and separated myself from the marriage. In retrospect, it probably ought not to have been so difficult, or prolonged. We take our lumps with sugar and move on, right? Apparently, but I didn't get that memo. For whatever reasons, I dragged the unhealthiness of my conflicting feelings far longer than was needed. In my case, the conflicting feelings centered on my desire to honor the commitment, to do the right thing – whatever that was, to avoid being a failure, to avoid hurting someone, and also around my profound sadness at the forever loss of connection with another family that I valued being a part of.

But, as I continue to learn with all difficult experiences, if one is open to the possibility that some meaning or lesson can be taken, then there can be a harvest of new growth in time.

A year or so before things ended, we attended a several day workshop put on by the Gottmans. Dr. John Gottman is a psychologist at the University of Washington. He and his team conduct research into the behavior of couples that seeks to predict whether a marriage will succeed or fail, and they have a high rate of success (94% accuracy) in their predictions. (Gottman, John. 1994. Why Marriages Succeed or Fail.) There must have been several hundred couples in attendance that weekend. I imagined they were struggling too. Looking around, it was easy to see that marital disharmony does not happen only to "bad" people. To the contrary, marriages among the best of people have conflict. What is important, say the Gottmans, is "compatibility", the fundamental personality attributes of each partner. The fireworks of this insight brought a sense of relief that I could dispense with guilt or blame because the problems and issues within my marriage weren't my fault, or my partner's. Rather, the failure of my marriage was the product of fundamental incompatibilities between two otherwise decent and responsible people, both of whom wanted the marriage to work, but who, for reasons mostly beyond their otherwise well-intentioned control, were likely fated to fail. We were good people, but very different and, ultimately, poorly matched.

I also learned that, according to Dr. Gottman, there are four attitudes (the Four Horsemen of the Marital Apocalypse), found to predict relationship failure. When these attitudes are present in a relationship, especially when there is more than one, there is a good chance the relationship will not survive. They are: criticism (finding fault or judging unfairly); contempt (disdain or scorn); defensiveness; and stonewalling and avoidance (withdrawing to avoid conflict). I could see aspects of these attitudes in my marriage, and ultimately determined they were significant enough that the marriage could never be a healthy one. In the end, the deck was stacked against us. How, without understanding the notion of fundamental compatibility in this way, could I have possibly made the right decision about a life partner back when I didn't know who I was or what I, or we, needed? Trial and error is not a very efficient process for forever-lasting marriages, as is proved by the fact that more than fifty percent of first-marriages end in divorce.

So, what then of romance? Well I assure you that, for me, romance is not dead; far from it. I hope to always hold on to that romantic ideal, and chase it to the sunset and beyond. But, I will choose to be, without judgment of the differences, more aware and mindful of the fundamental needs, requirements and attributes that are necessary components for a healthy relationship.

The Jumper

So this is what it feels like, falling through a cloud, Ben thought. He had always wanted to free-fall, and now, here he was, miles high, being pulled in the only direction gravity would allow. In the distance he could see two of the other jumpers, and the sun's glint reflecting off the plane's wing. He wondered what they were thinking, those two, and if he would get the opportunity to do this again then quickly dismissed the thought. He had responsibilities. A family, Chloe and Sara, waiting at the airport. Deadlines looming on the Halcyon merger. His annual physical.

Down below, the well-manicured fields, chalk shades of green and brown, went as far as he could see in every direction. How far away is the horizon at this altitude, he wondered. Fifteen, twenty, thirty miles? Funny, he thought, how some farms were square, some perfectly round, and how the river and roads made irrigation and commerce possible. He remembered the thought he had, looking out the window just after takeoff – how it never seemed to end, how up here you could see evidence of mankind, somewhere, all the time.

He noticed that his face and hands felt warm, but his eyes were stinging. Still, he didn't want to close them, so much to see, and so little time. There was just a whisper of sound. He had thought it would be louder, and imagined something like a wind tunnel. He was surprised his stomach didn't have the feeling like you sometimes get on a roller-coaster or on the big hill back home, the one that always made Chloe giggle when they drove over the crest. He spun lazily, looked skyward, breathed deeply then spun again. It was surprisingly easy to move this way and his body held no tension.

The ground was getting closer now and he started to count down from ten. His hand reached for the rip-line, then hesitated. He knew it would find emptiness. He looked down, felt the air on his lips, then on his teeth as he broke into a wide grin. He tried to whistle but the sky swallowed the sound. His thoughts drifted, and he worried for a moment about his laptop, still on the plane, and the data for the presentation – so many months of long hours and hard work. He wondered about his suitcase and the teddy bear for Chloe stowed on-board, and then saw the plane again. It looked smaller, its trajectory now nearly vertical, the trailing smoke thick and more evident than before. It surprised him that the plane would reach the ground before he did and he wondered if he would hear the explosion from the impact. He said a silent prayer for the passengers who had stayed, frozen in their fear. And he wondered what he would feel, if he would feel, when the earth came up to meet him.

Who Says There Are No Stupid Questions?

You've heard it said "There are no stupid questions, only stupid answers". Well, I beg to differ, having uttered several of the most stupid questions you can imagine. Here are four unforgettable stupid questions I've asked:

How many people did you kill? It was 1974, and springtime in the orange groves of Central Florida. I was fifteen. Nixon will resign in August, bringing end to an era. Coincidentally, I will get drunk for the very first time that same night, help cause some minor property damage, pass out, and wake up to the bold headline "Nixon Resigns". The war in Vietnam ended the year before. The fall of Saigon would not happen for another year. I was invited, along with a group of classmates, for dinner to the home of a teacher at our school. That teacher had been a fighter pilot in Vietnam. He displayed a framed picture of the fighter jet he flew on combat missions. Those who heard it said I asked a stupid question.

Are you expecting? It was 1981, summer, and a sunny day in Seattle. I was twenty-two and journey bound for law school in a month's time. The Reagan era had begun. The first space shuttle had been launched. The CDC would report the first five cases of AIDS. Charles and Diana would marry. MTV will air. The IBM PC will debut. Justin Timberlake, Britney Spears, Paris Hilton, and Beyonce' are born. I had been at the wedding of a fraternity brother. Later, at the reception I was talking with another "frat bro" and his cute but pooch-bellied wife. No one said it then, but I asked a stupid question.

How can you call yourself a virgin? It was 1984, the year of the Summer Olympics in Los Angeles; of Bernard Goetz; Vanessa Williams; the Apple Macintosh; and Bhopal, the worst industrial disaster in history.

It was mid-October, sunny and warm on the Greek Island of Naxos. I was twenty-five, had graduated from law school, taken the bar exam, and was nearing the end of a three-month adventure through Europe. My career lay ahead of me. I rented a motorcycle and spent the day navigating the island, met a nice American girl at the popular Agi Anna beach, and we hit it off. I invited her to ride with me the ten or so miles back into town. We had a nice dinner, according to my journal, and drank a bottle of Demestica, a light white wine from the neighboring island of Santorini. In the way that can happen to intrepid travelers, we decided to team up and make our way to Turkey, destination Istanbul. Our first stop was Santorini where we explored for several days, probably drinking more Demestica. Our next way-point was Mytilini (home of the lyric poet Sappho), fourteen hours via overnight ferry. They only had deck-class seats for purchase, but somehow, once aboard, my new friend managed to procure us a first-class stateroom. It's probably no surprise that we found ourselves with passionate feelings toward each other that soon blossomed into more than feelings. Somewhere along the way to Mytilini, in a small but cozy stateroom on a ferry on the Aegean Sea, I was pretty certain I asked a stupid question.

Will you marry me? It was 1994, the infamous year of O.J. Simpson, Tonya Harding and Lorena Bobbitt. The place: the Central American island of Roatan, Honduras. I was thirty-five. We were scuba-diving alongside a coral reef thirty-five feet underwater. An engagement ring had been securely placed in a small plastic-jeweled treasure chest like you might find in a tropical fish tank, had been hidden in the reef, and was waiting to be discovered. The fateful interrogatory had been written out on a slate designed for underwater writing. Sometime in the ten years that followed it would become evident that I had asked a stupid question.

Writing this, I've had time to reflect, and the more I ponder, the more I come to believe that maybe there really are no stupid questions, and the reason is "context". So I wanted to explore the nature of context. I wanted to know, exactly, what context is. The first place I looked was the Merriam-Webster Online Dictionary. Context is a thing, a noun, but not something you can hold in your hand. It is derived from Latin, and the etymology is mid-16th Century English. In Latin it means to "weave together a connection of words". But for anyone, except perhaps the Romans, that isn't much of a help, is it? It went further, saying "the parts of a discourse that surround a word or passage and can throw light on its meaning". Sorry Merriam-Webster, but that's not particularly helpful either.

If anything, that definition confuses me. I wanted more. I navigated to Wikipedia, or more accurately, Wikipedia's "Wiktionary" and found what is, for me, a more user-friendly definition: "the surroundings, circumstances, environment, background, or settings which determine, specify, or clarify the meaning of an event". You might say that sounds like something written by a lawyer but, okay, "circumstances" that clarify meaning. I get it.

I didn't need to go to these lengths to know what "context" means but thought it would be a good exercise to return to my stupid questions and imagine a circumstance where the question might not have been so stupid after all, in the proper context. I'll spare the details – the exercise was for my entertainment. But I will offer the insight that, for me, context is just another way of saying "think before you speak". On that, I thought it might be enlightening to navigate further into the Web for more helpings of wisdom. I found three sayings that offer a variety of perspectives on the theme.

"It's better to stay silent and look a fool, rather than speak and remove all doubt." Mark Twain, Benjamin Franklin, Abraham Lincoln

"Live your questions now, and perhaps even without knowing it, you will live along some distant day into your answers". Rainier Maria Rilke

And, poetically,

"I've learned that people will forget what you said, people will forget what you did, but people will never forget how you made them feel". Maya Angelou

Thank goodness for people forgetting the "what you said" part.

Please Get Checked (Early Detection Saves Lives)

March is National Colorectal Cancer Awareness Month.

It's not a fun topic, but if you read only one post from me, this is the one that matters most. Why is this important? It's important because colorectal cancer can happen even if you have no family history and no high-risk behaviors or habits like smoking or excessive drinking. It can happen even if you exercise regularly, get plenty of calcium, limit your intake of red meats, and eat plenty of fruits, beans and leafy vegetables.

It can happen at any age, to anyone. It can happen to a person who is in good health and not overweight. It can happen before the age of 50, and it can happen even if you work in a profession that well-understands the fact that doctors make mistakes.

Please pay attention to your body. See your doctor if you have any unusual changes, signs or symptoms. Second opinions are worth the time and effort when it's your life.

You need to know the signs and symptoms of colorectal cancer.

They are:

____ Rectal bleeding or blood in or on the stool

____ Change in bowel habits or stools that are narrower than usual

____ Stomach discomfort (bloating, fullness or cramps)

____ Diarrhea, constipation or feeling that the bowel does not empty completely

____ Weight loss for no apparent reason

____ Constant fatigue

____ Vomiting

Early detection is everything. Early detection will save your life.

All that follows below is shamelessly taken from readily available information online.

About Colorectal Cancer

Introduction

Colorectal cancer is cancer of the colon or rectum. It is equally common in men and women. An estimated 146,970 people were diagnosed in 2009, and an estimated 49,920 people died from the disease. With recommended screening, this cancer can be prevented (by removing polyps before they become cancerous) or detected early, when it can be more easily and successfully treated.

At Risk

____ Men and women age 50 and older

____ People who use tobacco, are obese or are sedentary

____ People with a personal or family history of colorectal cancer or benign (not cancerous) colorectal polyps

____ People with a personal or family history of inflammatory bowel disease, such as long-standing ulcerative colitis or Crohn's disease

____ People with a family history of inherited colorectal cancer

Risk Reduction

____ Be physically active and exercise regularly.

____ Maintain a healthy weight.

____ Eat a high-fiber diet rich in fruits, vegetables, nuts, beans and whole grains.

____ Consume calcium-rich foods like low-fat or skim milk.

____ Limit red meat consumption and avoid processed meats.

____ Don't smoke.

____ Don't drink alcohol excessively.

Early Detection

If you are at average risk for colorectal cancer, start having regular screening at age 50. If you are at greater risk, you may need to begin regular screening at an earlier age. The best time to get screened is before any symptoms appear. Use this guide to help you discuss screening options with your health care professional.

Consider one of the following:

Screening intervals for tests that find pre-cancer and cancer:

Colonoscopy: Every 10 years

Virtual colonoscopy: Every 5 years

Flexible sigmoidoscopy: Every 5 years

Double-contrast barium enema: Every 5 years

Screening intervals for tests that mainly find cancer:

Fecal occult blood test (FOBT): Every year

Fecal immunochemical test (FIT): Every year

Stool DNA test (sDNA): Ask your health care professional

Any abnormal result of a virtual colonoscopy or double-contrast barium enema, as well as a positive FOBT, FIT or sDNA test, should be followed up with a colonoscopy.

Life is precious. A healthy life is a treasured gift. Early screening is a healthy decision. Listen to your body, be mindful and see your doctor immediately. Be assertive and seek a second opinion. Give yourself and others the gift of your long and healthy life.

What's In A Nickname?

Crumplet. Crumper. Crumpster. Crumley. Crumplestiltskin. Crumpleminz. Corky. DC. Davido. Dave. Big Dave. Spud. Little Spud. Little Fella. Little Feller. Bubba. Huck. Razzmatazz. Honey Bunnie. Big Wally. Weetie. Weetness. Cheeks. Bumcheeks. Zebco. Zebedee. Zebediah. I've had a few nicknames in my life. Some have been conferred upon me by well-meaning folks who love or loved me, others by less-than-well-meaning individuals. As you can imagine, I prefer some of the pet-names over others.

Thinking about these sobriquets has me wondering about the circumstances that led to their evolution, and what, if anything might be learned from them. It also has me wondering if I have any favorites and, if so, why.

As I look over this list, what stands out are the time frames in my life where the nicknames were given or evolved. For example, the less-than-imaginative Crumplet, Crumper, Crum-Bum, Crumpster and Crumley all originated in college, by fraternity brothers. I guess there is no end to the creative impulses of intoxicated collegians. I'm willing to bet that my Dad (Big Ed, Eddie) shared the experience of being called something similar, back in the day when he was a fraternity man or in service during the war.

The endearing Weetie, Weetness, Cheeks, Boomis and Bumcheeks all sprouted up early during my marriage and were the source of genuine laughs and tenderness at the time. One of the best chuckle-fests I ever had came from the pillow-talking evolution of Weetie into Weetness Q. Bumcheeks. That's probably too much information, but a laugh is a laugh. I'm sure our friends and families experienced a gag-reflex every time they had to listen to one or both of us use those terms of endearment. I do, now.

The Spuds and Fellers come courtesy of my honorable friend and neighbor, Sir David the Lyman Hearted, aka Lymo aka Dee Ell (nicknaming goes both ways), a literal literary champ.

Zebco and its biblical iterations came from merciless summer camp kids. I had the good fortune to attend summer camp almost every year from first grade through seventh or eighth. I had the less-than-good-fortune to show up at Eagle's Nest Young Sportsman's Camp in Punta Gorda, Florida (a fishing, hunting, archery, riflery, ping-pong, snipe hunt and bug-juice paradise) bearing a wide grin of anticipation and sporting my new Zebco brand fishing rod and reel, only to learn that Zebco equipment was considered the brand of sissies by real sportsmen (or sports kids). In no time I was derisively christened Zebco, and the nickname stuck for four summers. Kids can be cruel. But I suppose they were just being honest. What's more, even after I begged, pleaded and cajoled my Dad into buying me a classier Mitchell brand fishing outfit, they called me Zeb just the same, thank you very much.

Corky and Razzmatazz were my own ill-fated attempts at forging a new identity, and both of them were dismal failures, thank goodness. Razzmatazz morphed, as you can imagine, into Razzmaspazz thanks to several nine- and ten-year old cabin mates at yet another summer camp in Deerwoode, North Carolina. I think we may have had too much time on our hands, or too much sugar from all the Captain Crunch we could eat and the peanut brittle, licorice and pudding cups (anyone remember Shake-a-Puddin?) from the care packages Mom would send. Corky, well, I don't even want to go there (think Dorky).

Bubba was conceived by a colleague (Tonto) who just believes we need nicknames. I like this one, though for some reason I think he should be the one called Bubba. He won't change with me though. I'd love to tell you the joke that these particular nicknames come from. Unfortunately, it's not fit for the general public.

Big Dave, perhaps my favorite, seems to re-emerge every few years in different settings. It first came about in Brussels or Bruges (Belgium). My recollection is dim (Belgian beer is good, and we were chasing every girl we met at the time) but I seem to recall that my friend, Big Pat, and I were hanging out with a couple of pals, one of whom was named Dave as well. We called him Super Dave just to keep things straight. More than twenty years later, a girlfriend's seventeen-year old daughter and her school friends started calling me Big Dave. I loved it. I felt honored that teens would validate me in this way. At least I think they were validating me. It's entirely possible that I'm out of touch and they were just making fun.

Some nicknames come and go, destined to live for only the instant moment. Those often show up attached to some combination of Sir and Frankenstein and Herr and Meister (Sir Crumpenstein or Herr Crumpelmeister). In a pinch, you can always start with "O" and an apostrophe, followed by the name and something Irish-sounding. For example, O'Crumpihan or O'Crumpessy would have been timely on Saint Patrick's Day.

Nicknames can be fodder for budding poets. I'm pretty sure that the kid who came up with Crumper-Dumper matriculated to academia. He entertained an easily amused classroom of first-graders with this rhyme: "Crump has a bump on his rump in the city dump". Do you suppose he remembered me when he got tenure?

It seems to me that nicknames are a shorthand of expression, and a convenient way to identify the dynamics of a relationship in just a word or two. I think that's because of the familiarity intended and engendered by a nickname. It's unlikely you'll get a nickname from anyone that you don't know, good or bad. However, there's no guarantee you'll get a nickname you like, even if it's given by someone who loves you. For example, my neighbor St. Elizabeth, who has known me for a decade-and-a-half, decided early in my illness to call me Crumley. I don't know what is intended by it, what it means, or how it came about, and honestly, I am not crazy about it as an endearment. Sorry St. E. But I can live with it, considering that a Saint, and dear friend, anointed me.

So, in answer to the question "What's in a nickname?" I think of familiarity, creativity, emotion, power, affection, love, humor, cruelty, irony, desire, ridicule, embarrassment, identity, identification, laughter, and friendship. I'm certain this just touches the surface, as there are probably as many reasons for a nickname as there are nicknames and persons to give or receive them. I wonder what the next nickname will be, who will give it, and why.

The Sin (?) Of Pride

I'm troubled. Why is Pride a sin, and a deadly sin at that? I work reasonably hard to earn a living, but also work, and play, so that I can take pride in my accomplishments. I work, in part, to be proud of who and what I am. Is it so wrong to have pride in one's self? I wouldn't think so, and my trusted "gut" agrees with me. But apparently, at least according to Christian theology, I'm dead (deadly sin) wrong.

Indeed, Pride (aka Hubris) is often considered to be the original and most serious of the seven deadly sins, and the source from which all other sins arise. I don't want to believe this, but I am compelled to remain open to the possibility that the Christian theologians might be right, or at least have thought this through. But to my way of thinking, other sins like Lust, Gluttony, Greed and Wrath would seem deadlier, just on their face. And yet, according to

Peter Binsfeld's Classification of Demons (1589) Pride is paired up with the demon Lucifer. Does it get any more demonic and sinful than that?

Encarta's English Dictionary seems to be on my side, defining Pride first as "satisfaction with self" and "the happy satisfied feeling somebody experiences when having or achieving something special that other people admire" and second as a "proper sense of own value", i.e. "the correct level of respect for the importance and value of your personal character, life, efforts, or achievements". But then Encarta brings me down with this, the third definition, a "feeling of superiority" and "a haughty attitude shown by somebody who believes, often unjustifiably, that he or she is better than others". Thanks Encarta, for bursting my bubble of relief. Still, I hardly see how Pride, even when it "goeth before a fall", is a sin, much less a deadly one.

It's challenging. Look up Pride in a thesaurus and you'll find "arrogance", "satisfaction" and "self-respect". Talk about a range on the spectrum. Can it be that everyone else is just as confused about this as I am?

The Roman Catholic Church, and most world religions call Pride a "sin of the intellect", while Aristotle considered Pride a "profound virtue". How then, do we reconcile the conflict? The answer, apparently, depends on who is being asked, and whether Pride is viewed as a virtue (temperance) or as a vice (excess, vanity). Virtue? Vice? It seems to me that the answer rests on who is making the judgment. And that places me in an uncomfortable position. I want to stand boldly, proudly, beside Aristotle, but there is a part of me that is afraid to challenge the religions. After the experiences I've had over the last several years, I surely do not want to incur the ire, wrath or judgment of Father, Son or Holy Ghost.

There does seem to be one safe harbor for me though, while I sort this question out to the extent I am able, and it rests in Pride's corresponding virtue, "Humility". I've long believed that Humility is one of my saving graces. Wikipedia defines Humility as "the quality of being modest, not proud, doing something out of the goodness of your heart, not for yourself". In various interpretations, Humility, as a philosophical or religious virtue, is seen as being connected with notions of transcendent unity with the universe or the divine, and of egolessness. Humility is said to be the foundation of spirituality, and inferior only to "faith", the first virtue, in as much as it removes the obstacles to faith and makes a person a fit recipient of grace. St. Bernard says that "Jesus Christ is the ultimate definition of humility". St. James says "God opposes the proud but gives grace to the humble". Good news then, as Humility (to the extent I possess it) would seem to be a fine and ready arrow in my soul's quiver as I do, genuinely, aspire to the notion and attainment of grace. But, by marked contrast, some schools of thought (Individualists, for example, who value the excellence of the individual) are sharply critical of humility. Nietzsche wrote of humility as a weakness, one that his Übermensch (Overman or Superman) would have considered pretentious, and a false virtue.

Well, I remain perplexed, no further along, perhaps, than when I began this essay. There seems to be a radical division on the subject, and all I can do to answer the question, for my own self, is straddle the philosophical and theological fences and remark "it depends".

No Quarter

The year is 1968 and I am 9 years old, a tanned and chubby third-grader in my uniform of gray slacks and white shirt (with blue blazer and navy blue clip-on tie on Fridays) at Pine Crest School in Fort Lauderdale, Florida. It is, in many ways, a difficult year, and I am struggling with my teacher, Mrs. H, who seems to not like me very much. I am a better than average student, but have classroom conduct problems, and at least twice this year I have been sent to the principal's office. For whatever reason, I learn much later on in life that my parents are asked that I not return the following year. I must have been someone's problem.

Our house sits on two gentle acres in Davie, a smallish western-themed South Florida town, charming in its way with wooden sidewalks and real honest-to-goodness hitching posts. I don't remember seeing any horses hitched to the posts, but it's not unusual to see horseback riders along the sides of the road on any given day and, indeed, we have two horses corralled in the back acre. I think one of them came with the house, and he throws me most times when I try to ride him. We have a dog, a cuss of a dachshund with the less-than-imaginative name of Snoopy. He bites me more than any kid's dog ought to. Teacher, horse, dog … it seems I am having trouble getting along. And I may not be the only one. It is, after all, 1968, a troubled year for America, and the Summer of Love is a memory (not that I know much of anything about it). The anthem of the day is from the Broadway musical Hair and I'm encouraged to let the sun shine in, on my long beautiful hair, in the dawning of the Age of Aquarius. But that won't be me. I'm no hippie. I have a crew cut, and my musical tastes run to the pop of Burt Bacharach, Sergio Mendes, Tom Jones, Spanky and Our Gang, and The Royal Guardsmen.

But despite the tumult of the times, there are good things to look forward to each day. I know my Mom and Dad love me. I have the freedom to go fishing at a little pond just down the road, with my cane-wood pole and a piece of bread for bait. I read plenty of books (Uncle Remus is a favorite, as is Homer Price). And I watch Mr. Rogers' Neighborhood on the brand new "fourth" network, PBS, most days after school on our black-and-white television (with rabbit ears wrapped in aluminum foil). Mom and I watch The Avengers every week, and thrill for the hour to the cool British Spy-fi crime-busting exploits and karate chop moves of Steed and the ever-so-lovely (indeed "sexy") Mrs. Emma Peel. As a family we love those Beverly Hillbillies and Agents 86 and 99. And I'm pretty sure that Mom and Dad like The Dick Van Dyke Show best of all.

But there is trouble being cooked-up on my horizon, and its names are Temptation and Larceny. I have appetites, literally, and soon I will lose a vestige of my youthful innocence and bear the shame of a common criminal.

My allowance is thirty-five cents a week. I'm not very good at saving it, and even if I was I don't really know what I would save for. Comic books quickly eat up whatever money I do have. Spiderman tops the list, but Daredevil is a close runner-up. He is a lawyer, after all. But there are other things that I want, like a plastic camera that sells for a dollar at the store. I suppose that's worth a month's allowance, but who has the patience for that? There is a plastic pencil-case that calls to me from a classmate's cubby, and there are MoonPies, delicious MoonPies whose wrappers smile at me day-after-day from the Canteen window after school ... a taste of heaven for only twenty-five cents. And twenty-five cents might just as well be a fortune to me. But I have a plan, and it might be foolproof. You see my Dad collects quarters. He has three sturdy collectible books of them, and for whatever reason he's put them in a drawer in the bureau in my room for safekeeping.

Now I don't know this in 1968, but MoonPies ("Just Right for Any Appetite") have a storied history. They were first made in Chattanooga, Tennessee in 1917 for coal miners who wanted something solid and filling that they could eat on-the-go because they didn't get much time for lunch. Mr. Earl Mitchell, Sr. had the idea of adding a coating of chocolate and a second cookie to graham cookies that were dipped into marshmallow. This "biggest snack on the rack" pleased the miners, and with a 10 ounce RC Cola (the MoonPie and the Cola each just a nickel) the "working man's lunch" was born. Later, they will serve the War effort, when hundreds of thousands of them are shipped to servicemen and women overseas.

At Mardi Gras, literally millions of MoonPies are thrown from floats every year, and they were, for a time, the "official snack cake" of NASCAR.

Well, though Eve didn't tempt Adam with a MoonPie, I'll bet it would have worked. And MoonPies ("Great for Kids, and for the Kid in All of Us") are tempting me in 1968. I am no match. Do I know that I will pay a price? I think not. Surely Dad won't miss one of the many quarters (about $1.52 in today's dollars). I reach into the bureau drawer for the handsome collectible books and gaze hungrily at the shiny round coins, the profiles of George ("I cannot tell a lie") Washington neatly arranged, year-by-successive-year. I pop out one of the newer quarters from its slot, aware on some level that the older ones have more value in the collection. And with that, I know there will be a MoonPie for me tomorrow… and the next day… and the next after that. With this scheme there will be MoonPies forever. I'll just take quarters randomly from each of the books so that none appear to be missing. I return again and again to the scene of the crime. But the MoonPies, chocolate, vanilla, and banana, they are what make the trials and tribulations of this unpleasant school year palatable. The crunch of the graham. The yield of the soft and chewy marshmallow. The sugary sweetness of the thick, generous flavor coating. Soon my greed overwhelms me, and I crave more than just MoonPies. I steal not one but four quarters for the camera. I steal my classmate's pencil box. Who knows what else I am laying my grubby little fledgling criminal mitts on? My day of reckoning is just around the corner. Still, I am surprised when it comes. But I cannot tell a lie either.

I have no excuse and no alibi for the larceny. Dad has me dead to rights and now it's time to pay for my crime. All criminals, except perhaps powerful corporations, must answer to the law. But I don't expect what happens next. Mom and Dad turn me in. And before I know it there is, yes, Johnnie Law, a policeman at the house. I see his cruiser pull up the drive. He steps inside, and I watch Mom and Dad as they pull away in their car. The policeman and I sit alone together in the quiet house and I hear him ask me if I want to go to jail. I hear myself answer, meekly, and honestly, "no". Is there any greater thing for a nine-year old to be afraid of than going to jail? One doesn't imagine such things as catastrophes at that age, but having played cops-and-robbers long before then, and watched plenty of westerns, I know what going to jail means, and in my mind it's surely worse than any catastrophe.

Looking back on that experience, I honestly don't remember what my punishment was. I'm not even certain that Mom and Dad knew about the MoonPies. I know that I received counseling from a child psychologist (aka the Heavenly Stargazer), so I felt a stigma from that, at the least.

I brought all this up while talking to my Dad the other day and he reminded me of something I had forgotten, that his collectible coins weren't just any quarters. Many, if not most of them, were silver quarters. Silver quarters were issued from 1932 to 1964. They are 90 percent silver and ten percent copper. At today's prices, the total melt value for a silver quarter is $3.23 (per the Silver Coin Melt Value Calculator). And of course, some years have more "mintage" value than others. For example, the 1932 D and S coins have a numismatic value that ranges from $200 to a staggering $15,000. Even the 1964 mintage has a numismatic value as high as $30. That's a lot of MoonPies, at any price.

Well Dad, I owe you my thanks for not sending me to jail, and a Moon-sized apology. We'll never know just how much it cost you to satisfy my cravings. You said that you never sweated the episode very much. Maybe you were just relieved that I didn't join the Moonies (okay, lousy pun). But still, a man has to make amends. I estimate having taken twenty or so quarters from your books during the silver spree. I can't factor the numismatic value, or afford to, but I can calculate the Coin Melt Value. At $3.23 per silver quarter I figure to owe you, conservatively, $64.60 and I'm sending you a check for that amount immediately (or the equivalent in MoonPies, it's your call. They can ship directly from Chattanooga in a personalized box).

Oh, and aside from the obvious lesson that crime doesn't pay, the other lesson here is this: parents, increase your kids' allowances and feed them plenty of tasty treats, or suffer the consequences at your peril.

Save The Last Dance

Each and every one among us surely wishes we might have the opportunity for a do-over or two in life. I have plenty of those wishes, and likely will have plenty more. Whether they spring from actions or inactions our choices, in large part, determine the course of our lives. I believe all that separates any of us are 1) opportunities and 2) choices. Life is constantly presenting opportunities and we are constantly making choices and some are better than others. Here's a story of opportunities presented and choices made, curious choices I as reflect on them. And as prom season nears, this story seems appropriate.

I was eighteen years old in April of 1977, springtime, and a senior at John I. Leonard High School in Lake Worth, Florida. It was a good year at a school I liked, with lots of sunshine, going to the beach after school with friends, and reasonable academic and social success. After years of climbing the ladder I finally felt included in the top of the high school social scene, the enviable "A-List". Things seemed so good that even my class-clown behavior went over well with most of my teachers and I had a good sense of how to be "cool". I guess I just felt liked. And with prom approaching, being liked was a pretty important thing.

The year before, as a junior, I went to the prom with a senior and she and I had a really good time. I'll never forget that prom, the bottle of champagne I managed to score earlier that day, or my date. She is a friend to this day and a reader of these blog essays on occasion. Maybe it was because we had such a good time that I didn't feel a strong desire to attend the prom my senior year. I didn't have a girlfriend either so there wasn't much of any felt pressure to go. Basically it just wasn't all that important to me, at the time.

But what did seem important, and I really don't understand why, looking back on it, was Florida's annual Senior Night at Disney World. That event was open to every senior in the State of Florida. Seniors would bus in from all corners and the park would be open until the early hours. Bands would play (KC and the Sunshine Band and Starbuck ("Moonlight, Feels Right") that year) and tens of thousands of 17 and 18 year olds would be doing what they do.

So I made a choice and chose Senior Night over prom. Flash forward to Senior Night… it turned out to be a bore. Everyone else I knew there had a date. I felt awkward and lonely among my peers and recall asking myself why I was doing this. I couldn't wait for it to end. There's a word for the choice I made and that word is "dumb". But the story doesn't end there.

Rewind to the two or three weeks before prom. Two things stand out. The first is that my Mom casually mentioned that her friend's daughter, let's call her "C", didn't have a date to the prom. It doesn't take a rocket scientist to know that Mom was looking out for me and that she got her information from a reliable and motivated source. What did I do? Instead of saying "Hey, thanks for the hot tip Mom" I grumbled something about not needing any help in my social life thank you very much. I'm sure that hurt Mom's feelings and it also kept me from having a presumably memorable night at the prom with C, a very pretty and sweet girl. I was looking at her yearbook picture just the other day. We would have had fun.

The other choice made a week or so later also stings. Prom night was getting closer, and I imagine some of those girls who didn't have dates were feeling a bit anxious. One of them, another very pretty and sweet girl "D" (again, her yearbook picture proves it) walked up to me by our lockers and shyly asked if I would go to the prom with her. She must have been nervous. I would have been. It was sincerely flattering to be asked and it came out of the blue. I remember my answer clearly, "Thank you D, but I'm not going to the prom". She probably didn't expect that. Maybe if I had more time to consider her invitation in advance my answer, my choice, would have been different. One can only hope.

Well, for whatever reason, the choices were made. C and D found dates. The weekend of the prom came and went. I remember driving around that Saturday night when most of my friends were engaging in that annual rite of passage and feeling lonely, a bit foolish, and wondering what I was missing.

On Monday morning I found out exactly what I missed. My lovely D had been elected Prom Queen. She didn't rub in the egg that was clearly on my face though. If anything, when we inevitably passed each other by our lockers she gave me a look that I interpreted as "What were you thinking, you sweet misguided boy?" Ouch! It still hurts, even thirty-three years later, and every time I see prom kids this time of year, all dressed up and having fun, I visualize what it might have been like to promenade with C or D. I coulda' been a contender.

Opportunities presented and choices made. Sure, I was only eighteen years old then, not very smart, and I had my reasons. Maybe in some grand cosmic scheme they were even the "right" choices. I'll never know for certain. But I do know that I'd like a do-over. Maybe the best I can hope for is that C and D may someday learn about my regrets and know that it wasn't about them. I was just plain dumb, misguided, clueless. The choices were all mine, and having made them I get to slow-dance with their consequences for the rest of my life.

Power Of The Mind

In November of 2008 I found myself admitted back in the hospital for the sixth time that year. It had been a long eleven months of tests, diagnoses, surgeries, chemotherapy and radiation treatments, and I was becoming entirely too familiar with the rooms, hallways, nurses and staff on 8 West at Stevens Hospital. Fortunately, I've proved to be a pretty good patient, endeavoring to be "the best patient this hospital's ever seen", and though frustrating, time-consuming, scary and anxiety-producing, if you need to get well, there are worse places to be than a good hospital.

This time around I was admitted for what was my second bout with small bowel obstruction, a recognized consequence of abdominal surgery. As a surgical residual, obstructions are not pleasant. They can happen for a number of reasons: scarring; adhesions; inflammation; kinking; and twisting. They come on suddenly, a powerful kick in the gut that repeatedly spasms and worsens in duration and intensity until, eventually, if the obstruction doesn't clear you'll start throwing up, doubled over in agony. By then you're guaranteed a hospital admission and minimum three-day stay. If you're lucky the ER staff will give you a shot or two of Demerol. That will calm you down. Once admitted to the floor, a nurse will tether you to an IV line for fluids, and then another nurse will come into the room with a three-foot long naso-gastric tube and large plastic cup approximately the size of a Super Big Gulp. The nurse forcefully inserts the tube up and into a nostril, pivots and shoves the tube into your throat, and guides it down your esophagus, where it will eventually come to rest in your stomach. You will be told to keep swallowing, will gag reflexively and your eyes will tear up. The tender tissue inside your nostril will make a crunching sound as the tube, and its guided end make their way downstream.

Then the nurse will hook the tube to the large cup, plug the cup into a socket on the wall behind your head, and activate the suction that is designed to relieve the back-pressure on the obstruction. They call it decompression. The suction process can last for several days, as the nursing staff monitor whether the obstruction is clearing or not. You feel like the Elephant Man, or a damned rhinoceros, with the offensive tube curled a foot or so out in front of your face. It hurts to turn your head because the tube irritates your sensitive nostril, and every swallow is a constant reminder of the trespassing device. When you walk the corridors of the hospital floor little children look at you with curiosity, having never seen that before.

If the obstruction clears then you'll get started on a diet of clear liquids (broth and especially popsicles never tasted so good), advance to full liquids (cream soup, milk, pudding), then finally move on to solid food.

If the obstruction doesn't clear then you and your surgeon will make a date. That's what happened to me that week. After the fairly routine surgery I woke up in recovery and began the groggy, fuzzy re-orientation process that patients go through after coming out of general anesthesia. I'm always intrigued by that experience, waking up and trying to piece together the bits of my memory from the moments just before going under.

Back in my hospital room after surgery, the nurse pointed out that in addition to the fluids from my IV, I also had a PC, the little red button you can push that dispenses pain controlling medication, in my case Dilaudid, a synthetic form of morphine. I'd had the PC drip with the familiar red button after previous surgeries. It's designed so you can't get too much. No matter how much or how often you push the button, you only receive a small measured dose every ten minutes. Usually, in my case, the PC drip would be hooked up for two or three days. Everyone's different, with varying levels of pain tolerance.

As intended, when I pushed the PC button, as needed for pain, I would feel the predictable though temporary relief (minutes to hours). On the third day of my recovery the nurse came in to unhook the PC because my doctor had ordered a weaning switch to oral pain medication. I recall seeing my nurse at bedside, looking at the IV stand and the PC drip pump attached to it. She had a curious expression. She made a sound … "Huh". I asked her "What?" and she said, in her Caribbean lilt, "It's not hooked up". Indeed, my PC was never activated. Each and every time I pushed that little red button during those three days, thinking I was getting "dosed", I simply wasn't. And yet, I distinctly recall feeling the pain-reducing effect when I pushed the button. I even remarked on it occasionally. The doctors didn't intend for this to happen, as far as I know, but I experienced the "placebo effect" first-hand.

The placebo effect (in Latin – "I shall please") is a well-recognized phenomenon. At its most basic, a placebo is a deception, a sham intervention (whether substance or procedure) that can cause a patient to believe the treatment will change his or her condition. This belief can then produce a subjective perception of a therapeutic effect, causing the patient to feel that his or her condition has improved. It points to the importance of perception, and to the role of the brain, in maintaining physical health.

Body processes such as pain, motor fatigue and fever are directly organized by the brain. Other processes such as the immune system are also controlled indirectly through the sympathetic and parasympathetic nervous systems. Studies show that the brain has control, or in a conditioning environment can learn control, over these physiological processes.

In a curious twist, the nocebo effect (in Latin – "I shall harm") also exists. A patient who disbelieves in a treatment may experience a worsening of symptoms. Simply having a negative attitude towards the effectiveness of a treatment or substance prescribed can make a meaningful difference that interferes with a patient's ability to get well.

It's not my purpose or place to criticize the research and literature on placebo and nocebo effects. There is intense debate both as to the validity of placebo and nocebo effects and to their use in the health care setting, as well as whether it is ethical or not to administer a placebo to an unknowing or unsuspecting patient. But I leave those questions to the experts and ethicists. My purpose is simply to share a personal experience, and reflect on it. Early on, shortly after my diagnosis, a very good friend said these words. "Keep a positive mental attitude". I adopted his mantra… "PMA, Baby!" When times were tough that seemed to make a difference. Is it a real difference or one just perceived? Who's to say? All I can share is that it helped me through the day, much like another recognized phenomenon then and now, the "Momcebo" (the therapeutic and healthful benefits one gets from having a terrific Mom).

Happy Mothers' Day, Mom. You're the best, and I love you.

Sowing The Seeds

Last week I found myself doing something I really enjoy, eating ice cream in the middle of the day, specifically a chocolate cherry Blizzard at Dairy Queen. There happened to be a Little Nickel Classifieds paper on the table and I like to peruse the written word when eating alone. On the front page, boldly above the fold and in full color, were no less than four two-inch box ads for medical marijuana. It seems that the issues of decriminalization of marijuana for personal use and legalization of medical marijuana for legitimate medical purposes are more and more in the news, from the development of marijuana cultivation supply super-stores, to criminal busts and violent armed robberies of medical marijuana grow operations. Even a top-rated prime-time sitcom recently featured a story-line where the main character obtained an authorization for medical marijuana. When something becomes that mainstream then I believe it's a fairly safe assumption we'll be seeing and hearing a lot more about it. In other words, it's here to stay and not going away.

The medicinal value of marijuana is disputed but it does have several well-documented beneficial effects: the amelioration of nausea and vomiting; stimulation of hunger in chemotherapy and AIDS patients; lowered intra-ocular eye pressure (effective for treating glaucoma); and general analgesic effects.

There are important differences between medical marijuana at the federal and at the state levels. At the federal level, cannabis has been made criminal by implementation of the Controlled Substances Act which classifies marijuana as a Schedule I drug, the strictest classification.

On the state level, fourteen states and one district have legalized medical marijuana: Alaska, California, Colorado, Hawaii, Maine, Michigan, Montana, Nevada, New Jersey, New Mexico, Oregon, Rhode Island, Vermont, Washington D.C. and Washington. Six states currently utilize dispensaries. California's medical marijuana industry took in about $2 billion and generated $100 million in state sales taxes in 2008 with an estimated 2,100 dispensaries, co-operatives, wellness clinics and taxi delivery services in the sector appropriately known as "cannabusiness".

I'm not here to advocate for decriminalization, legalization or authorization, though as a generally untaxed and unregulated industry there is enormous potential for revenue generation in marijuana cultivation and distribution similar to what we have in this country with tobacco and alcohol. I just have a story to share.

In the springtime of 1977, in the sunny, warm and humid South Florida climate, I was eighteen years old, a high school senior, technically an adult but far from immune to peer pressure, and well, curious. Pot was readily available and it was not uncommon for some of my friends and classmates to smoke it. I will admit to having joined them on occasion. I don't recall my grades suffering and in a curious twist, I received nearly straight A's that year.

At some point I decided it might be an instructive experiment to grow a plant. I did just that, and planted the little brown seed in a moist and fertile medium in a small green plastic starter container placed prominently under the study light on the desk in my bedroom. I waited and watched over the days and weeks as the seedling germinated and first broke through the soil and then continued to grow … two inches … six inches. Before long the little plant was too big for the starter container, and my desk, so I re-potted it (no pun intended) and moved it outside, placing the healthy plant carefully in a ditch that ran alongside the property at 7 West Palm Avenue. More days and weeks went by and the plant reached a height of about forty inches. It was, indeed, high time to think about a harvest.

South Florida is known for its brief but torrential rainfall ("thunder-boomers" and "gully-washers" in the jargon of the local weatherpersons). Sure enough one day a torrent fell that caused local flooding. I knew that ditch alongside our house was flowing fast. All I could think about as I sat through classes and on the bus ride home was what fate had befallen the hardy plant that surely took a full brunt of the flood.

By the time I arrived home the ditch had cleared. The plant was knocked on its side, half out of its container, and covered with insects. Thankfully it had not washed away. I gently repacked the plant and picked off the insects one by one. In a flash of inspiration I remembered something my Dad had in the garage … a grow light that he must have used for his vegetable starters. I brought the plant into the house, placed it in my shower, suspended the grow light over the shower nozzle and aimed it at the plant. The powerful light lit up the small room. The plant could not have been happier, having had a good bath earlier in the day, a thorough grooming, and now a chance to soak up some warm, albeit artificial, rays.

Throughout the afternoon and evening I checked on the plant's progress and I do believe it grew more bushy by the hour. I went to bed that night, fully intending to move the plant back outside the next morning. I was in for a surprise.

I woke up and padded into the bathroom only to find the room was … dark. Still, I had hope, but when I peered into the shower stall my fears were confirmed. The plant and all evidence of it, was gone. I conducted a brief but pointless search, then showered and caught the bus to school. Mom and Dad must have slept through that part of the morning, or else they decided to avoid me then and deal with it later. And that's just what happened. Meanwhile, I had the distinctly unpleasant experience of going through the motions at school that day, and anticipating what wait in store for me at home that afternoon.

When I arrived home the house was empty. I sat at the kitchen table having a snack, waiting and wondering. Finally the front door opened. In they came, Mom and Dad, judge and jury. The moment of truth was at hand. No one was smiling. My mind must have been engaged in a hyper-calculus, attempting to assess the degrees of anger, disappointment and fear that we all must have been feeling. I recall Dad asking me some questions along the lines of what did I have to say for myself, and learning that he had woken in the middle of the night, seen the bright light shining out from under my bathroom door, become upset that I had left the light on (wasting electricity), discovered the plant (how could he miss it), identified it, and ... the horror ... destroyed it. Later on I learned he hated doing that because it was so darn green, bushy and healthy. I was a man after that gentleman farmer's heart. But what stands out much more clearly was that Mom seemed angrier than Dad, and this surprised me. She kept asking the question "Where did you get the seeds?" I recall thinking to myself what the heck difference did that make (though I dared not ask her that at the time).

I don't recall what punishment they gave. Probably I was grounded for a time. It wasn't a capital offense and I was eighteen after all. Back then it was legal for an eighteen year old to buy and drink alcohol in Florida. But what came out, as the days went by, was the story that when Dad showed Mom the contraband (while I was blissfully unaware in peaceful slumber) her response was "Oh how nice, Dave got me a plant for Mother's Day". And that was entirely reasonable, she being a Mom and it being the Friday before her special day. Dad replied "Honey, that's cannabis". Mom either didn't believe him, or more likely didn't want to believe him, and I reckon it may have been the disappointment that fueled her sense of betrayal and hurt.

This story is one that my Mom and Dad grew fond of telling their friends. It's been thirty-three years and they've gotten a lot of mileage from it. Somehow it touched us as a family...the contrasting notions of a Mother's instinctive belief that her Son had done something thoughtful for her, and the harsh disappointment upon learning that her Son had done something, well, criminal. What's wonderful is that the story became and still is a source of reflection and laughter for us. It's a fond reminder of a place and time and age when we were happy and life was a bit simpler, perhaps gentler. Just one month later I would graduate from high school. In three month's time I would be fully across the country at college. The house would be quieter. Mom and Dad would be "empty-nesters" and I would have little sense or appreciation of what that experience must have been like for them. It was a time of innocence, even in the bright light of that (albeit relatively minor) criminal act. Like the plant, I was growing, rapidly and strong. Like the plant, I needed to be out of the house. I've tried to find one, but don't believe there is any great moral or instructive lesson in this. It's enough that we as a family found humor in the situation. Maybe I can just end on this note (a mighty stretch, so please be kind): if you happen to discover that your kid is doing something similar to what I did back then, embrace the moment and celebrate it not as a tempest in a teapot, but as a hemp-fest in a green pot. (I told you it was a mighty stretch.)

A Review Of *Win Your Case*

For my lawyer friends and colleagues, I'd like to summarize Gerry Spence's *Win Your Case* (St. Martin's Press. Hardcover. 304 pages.)

• Tell the truth.

• Withhold permission to be defeated.

• Practice telling the story, paying attention to the "verbs".

• Discover the truth and story of the case by "becoming" the other (the client, adversary, judge, witness, juror).

• Find the theme.

• Brainstorm spontaneously.

Now this is not fair to Gerry Spence, or to any lawyer who believes they no longer need to read this book, because there is much more.

Mr. Spence also devotes attention to each part of a trial, from voir dire (jury selection) to closing argument, sharing his insights and knowledge gained from years of experience. But as it turns out, I'm not really here to talk about that.

I like Gerry Spence, once fully idolized him, and I am a true believer of his methods. I've read nearly everything he's written about the practice of law. I attended his Trial Lawyer's College for thirty amazing, mind opening days in August 1996; attended week-long Graduate programs; studied and participated in numerous workshops; peeled the layers of my own self's onion, right down to the core (but probably still not deeply enough); learned to appreciate the importance of being genuine, authentic and in the moment; allowed myself to get out of its all too familiar comfort zone; stood in the shoes of my client, and others; learned to care, and care deeply, about my clients; and risked myself, whether trying cases, trying new methods, or taking on new challenges.

Still, I struggle to become the truly great (there's that word again) trial lawyer I want to be, and continue to hope to be. I am no longer the youthful thirty- or even forty-something with the energy to devour every new book, attend every seminar or risk it all on every case. I also no longer believe that a book, or a hundred books, a seminar, or a hundred seminars can provide "the answer". Paradoxically, the more I read about trial skills and winning methods, the more questions I have. Sadly, there is no one great "pearl of wisdom", no "magic bullet" to greatness. I have learned that some who appear great may be little more than "paper tigers". A truly exceptional and proven lawyer whom I admire deeply, the great Paul Luvera of Seattle, said that anyone can be a paper tiger. That struck a resonant chord and it also made me feel small because I saw some of my own self in that comment. He's right, of course, and in the end what matters is the result.

I've had some successes in a minor key (though the successes pale in comparison to those of my "heroes" and quite a few peers) and gained valuable insights along the way. I am learning to be more relaxed in the courtroom (a decidedly un-relaxing place to be if ever there was one), though I didn't do that alone. I want to thank my friend and colleague Eric Fong for helping me discover my relaxed self in the stultifying atmosphere of the courtroom. In our collaborations, Eric helped teach me an even more valuable lesson and it is this: don't try so hard. It's easier said than done, however, and easier when you have a colleague like Eric watching your back when the trench warfare of the courtroom begins. It's also more fun. And even though war is bloody business, if you have to go you might as well have some fun if you can. This principle is echoed in Tim Gallwey's *The Inner Game of Tennis*. Gallwey's point is a paradoxical one; that the harder you try the worse you will do. He believes that we perform at our best when we are relaxed and when we let our natural instinctive self take over, doing what it knows how best to do, without interference from our critical ego.

I've had to come face-to-face with the fact of who I am; someone not really inclined to be confrontational by nature. I don't really care to argue much, nor do I do it very well. I recognize that conflict can be healthy, but for the most part I detest and revile that part of my profession that deals with conflict, in every case, on trivial after trivial matter, on a daily basis. I curse the conflict and the justice system for its inefficiencies, costs, delays, winner-take-all attitudes, ego-trips, power-trips, embarrassments, inconveniences, skirmishes, abuses and much more. Mostly, I detest the sometimes absurd lengths of time that are required for "justice" to be done in our system.

I could tell you about a recent case, at long last concluded, that spent ten years winding through the courts (Superior Court, Bankruptcy Court, the Court of Appeals, the State Supreme Court and back to Superior Court) before it settled and the exhausted client received her measure of justice for the carelessness of the doctor and the injuries he caused her more than thirteen years ago. I could tell you about another case, one in which my 77 year-old client was crossing the street and hit by a careless driver nearly seven years ago, his head smashing the windshield. He suffered a concussion and brain injury, can no longer volunteer his time and service, and is embarrassed, frustrated and forgetful. His wife of fifty years, who never drove a car and never balanced the family checkbook, now must cope and deal with his and her own residual frustrations. Together they and their family fight to save the family home from foreclosure. My client is daily aging, and patiently waiting for his day in court. His case has been continued four times. His case is scheduled for trial in July. It may yet be continued again, and neither he nor his attorneys have any say. There are just too many criminal cases in that county court; too few judges; and too few resources.

I've learned that the average individual, be they family, friend, neighbor or juror, knows very little of what goes on in the daily life or into the work of a plaintiff's lawyer. I understand this, and I am frustrated too. There is a great deal of open cynicism towards lawyers (especially trial lawyers), and the legal system. There is a great amount of distrust. We are no longer cloaked with the aura and respect of, say, an Abraham Lincoln, Atticus Finch or Clarence Darrow in the public mind. Sadly, I believe the public perceives us to be more like the ridiculous caricatures portrayed in Boston Legal. It's fairly well accepted that the perception of the credibility of trial lawyers among the general public is decidedly an unfavorable one, on par with, or a rung just above auto sales people. I imagine it's reflective of the times we live in, but it's unfortunate because it reflexively prejudices those who are wronged under our system of laws and who seek accountability and fair justice within that system.

It was not my purpose, at the outset, to rant. It does little good to spit in the wind or pee upstream. Rather, all I hope to do here is share how I feel, and hope that the light of my sharing brings some meaningful insight to my own way of doing and being, and some meaningful consideration to the notion that what we do as plaintiff's lawyers, in trial or out, is hard work for good people. There's a lot of genuine caring happening out there, in and out of the trenches, for deserving people.

One day you may find yourself sitting as a juror in judgment upon someone. If that happens, I ask you please to take a moment of pause, and though you may not want to think about it, reflect upon the notion, the possibility, that any one of us could be fitted for the shoes of the deserving some day.

(Note: I apologize that this essay lacks a coherent theme. It meanders too much and may not meet my standard. Unfortunately, I'm on a self-imposed deadline. Fortunately, I'm going fishing.)

Actions – Louder Than Words

I'm not a psychiatrist, psychologist or counselor, but as a trial lawyer I am required to invest considerable time learning about my client, learning about the other side, about the other side's lawyer, about the judge, and about the members of the jury. In the courtroom at the outset of a jury trial I am required to interact with as many as 40 or more potential jurors and make determinations about their character, values and suitability as a juror for the case in as few as thirty allotted minutes. As a human being involved in day-to-day interactions with family, friends and colleagues I'm also probably better off the more I know about the person I'm interacting with. The same goes for that person I see in the mirror every day; the more I know about myself the better, most likely. So the question is how do I go about learning as much as I can about the individuals I come into contact with, and myself, in the shortest time and in the most efficient manner? And how can I trust that the information and knowledge I do learn is accurate enough for me to rely on?

We are gifted by nature with five senses: touch; smell; taste; hearing; and sight. We are also gifted with the ability to communicate verbally (the spoken word) and non-verbally (the written word and our actions). I believe and I think it's obvious that if we want to "make sense" of our world or someone in it then we should use all of our senses to the best of our abilities. But I also believe that as humans, capable of error, prejudice and bias, we can be led astray and can lead ourselves astray in our thinking. For example, suppose I meet an individual and want to know more about him or her. I can simply ask the person to tell me about him or herself. Suppose the person complies, generously, and speaks a thousand words or more. Can I trust that information? Would it be better if I asked the same question to someone else or maybe even five other individuals who know the person; can I trust that information?

Eric Oliver, author of *Facts Can't Speak for Themselves*, and others have written that the majority of a person's mental processes are occurring outside of that person's conscious review or direction. In other words, though we may assimilate information, we are most likely unable to fully access that information. An example of this, taken from my line of work, happens after the trial when the attorneys canvass the jurors, soliciting their opinions and feedback. The attorneys typically ask the jurors for the reasons why they decided as they did, and the jurors, or some of them, will give their reasons. Unfortunately, because of their inability to access that part of the unconscious responsible for decision-making, the jurors themselves are unable to accurately answer the "why" question. To be sure, they will give answers. But the value of those answers is suspect. How often have you been asked and then answered a "why" question in such a manner as to protect yourself, someone else or the person asking the question? Even when you make conscious and valiant efforts to do so, it is difficult to be entirely truthful and accurate.

Here's another example, taken from personal experience. The other day I asked myself the question "What are the three things I value most?" Here's what I came up with, in this order: health; love for family; and security. But then I took a close look at my actions with regard to those values. If indeed it is the case that I value my health above all other things then why don't I eat better? How come I ate at McDonald's for breakfast a couple of times that week and the week before? Why the donuts for dessert? How come I'm not at the gym, on the treadmill for an hour a day, every day? How come I'm not going for walks on a regular basis? Why didn't I use sunscreen on that fishing trip or when working in the yard all weekend? Where are my eight glasses of water a day? Do you see what I mean? My actions give lie to the words. And without action, all the words in the world and the intentions behind them are nothing but a sham; an insidious misdirection. I can understand fooling others from time-to-time, but in this instance I was fooling myself.

Building on the excellent work of Clotaire Rapaille, author of *The Culture Code* (the Culture Code is the unconscious meaning we apply to any given thing), trial consultant David Ball and trial lawyer Don Keenan write about juror decision-making in *Reptile:*

The 2009 Manual of the Plaintiff's Revolution. Ball and Keenan make the case that we humans hold on to the notion, and like to believe that we are run by logic (the cognitive brain) and by emotion. While that is true to an extent, they assert that in a game of mental tug-of-war the Reptilian brain (the instinctive brain) wins out. The Reptilian brain is all about safety; our own safety and the safety of our propagated (offspring) or yet-to-be propagated genes. In instances of danger the Reptile within will firmly take control and act. And for the most part this happens outside of consciousness and conscious control. Rapaille states it boldly: "YOU CAN'T BELIEVE WHAT PEOPLE SAY". He writes: "This is not to suggest that people intentionally lie or misrepresent themselves. What it means is that, when asked direct questions about their interests and preferences, people tend to give answers they believe the questioner wants to hear. Again, this is not because they intend to mislead. It is because people respond to these questions with their cortexes, the parts of their brain that control intelligence rather than emotion or instinct. They ponder a question, they process a question, and when they deliver an answer, it is the product of the deliberation. They believe they are telling the truth. A lie detector would confirm this. In most cases, however, they aren't saying what they mean."

Rapaille goes on to say "The reason for this is simple: most people don't know why they do the things they do."

No, you can't believe what people say, but I do subscribe to the notion that, for the most part, you can believe what they do.

I will stand here for the proposition that if you really and truly want to learn about a person then you need to learn what it is that he or she "values", and that to learn what a person values there is no better way than to learn about what they "do". I don't mean "do" as in the work they perform at their job every day, though that can be important in its own right. Rather, I mean to say "do" as in their "actions". I believe that actions are the lever that opens the door to, and the spotlight that shines upon values. I say forget talk. Talk is cheap. Talk evaporates. But "doing" reverberates. "Doing" happens in the moment. "Doing" is action and actions speak louder than words because action requires effort (and often sustained effort). No wonder then that the expression "Talk is cheap" is so firmly entrenched in our language. This is also echoed in research positing that the verbal content of a presentation, the words themselves, account for only a small percentage of the persuasiveness of your message, to wit:

Your verbal ability, or your content and knowledge about your topic (i.e. the words you speak), counts for only 7 percent of the audience's perception of you.

Your vocal ability, or how you speak, including your tone, pitch and inflection (i.e. the sound of the words) counts for 35 percent of the audience's perception of you.

Your visual presence, or how you physically look (i.e. how you appear) while presenting, counts for a whopping 55 percent of the audience's perception of you.

In thinking about this, it strikes me just how many rock and roll and pop songs I have listened to over the years, hundreds and in some cases possibly thousands of times, enthusiastically, that I still don't know all the words to. Yet the songs move me, again and again.

Here's an exercise. Just look around. Carefully observe an individual in your surroundings. It could be a spouse, family member, friend, colleague or stranger. Observe with all of your senses as you ponder in your mind and feel in your gut what that person is doing right now or has done in the past to be who and where he or she is in this moment. Reflect on the choices that person is making or has made that led him or her to become that person. What do your observations tell you about that person's values?

It takes some effort to do this, and a bit of discipline to stay focused. It might help if you have taken time to familiarize yourself with one or more values lists. Keep in mind there are "values" and then there are the "fundamental values". For example, a person might value fidelity in a relationship. Fundamentally, that may suggest the person values "security" or "tradition" or "conformity". A person may value doing a good job at work. Fundamentally, that may suggest the person values "achievement" or "power". That's pretty important stuff to know, if you ask me.

There are hundreds of values, at least according to the "values list" at livingmore.org. But central to this discussion are the ten fundamental values identified by Rokeach, Schwartz, Williams, Kluckhohn and others. Each of the ten basic values is recognized in virtually every culture and each has a central motivational (and motivationally distinct) goal. They are:

Self-Direction — Independent thought and action; choosing, creating, exploring;

Stimulation — Excitement, novelty, and challenge in life;

Hedonism — Pleasure and sensuous gratification for oneself;

Achievement — Personal success through demonstrating competence according to social standards;

Power — Social status and prestige, control or dominance over people and resources;

Security — Safety, harmony, and stability of society, of relationships, and of self;

Conformity — Restraint of actions, inclinations, and impulses likely to upset or harm others and violate social expectations or norms;

Tradition — Respect, commitment, and acceptance of the customs and ideas that traditional culture or religion provide the self;

Benevolence — Preserving and enhancing the welfare of those with whom one is in frequent personal contact (the 'in-group'); and

Universalism — Understanding, appreciation, tolerance, and protection for the welfare of all people and for nature.

Why is it important to know what another person values? Because values are predictive of behavior. (See *Basic Human Values: An Overview*, by Shalom S. Schwartz.) I think any of us would be hard-pressed to argue against the utility and power, indeed the "value" inherent in accurate forecasting. I was in the room when the great Gerry Spence said "If you know what they value then you have them by the balls". He was referring to juries, and he ought to know. Many years later, in the process of winding down my marriage and working to sort through the reasons why I chose the marriage partner that I did (in the face of now and probably then-obvious red flags) a helpful counselor taught me this lesson: we make choices given the values we have at the time. That allowed me to understand why I overlooked (consciously or otherwise) those character traits that, combined with my own, led to fundamental marital incompatibilities.

We are what we value and we are what we experience (what we do and have done). We are the sum total of our experiences and actions. Values and experiences derive from action (or inaction, which is a form of action) and our choices. Our values shape the experiences we seek, and our experiences shape the values we desire. The next time you are interested in learning about a person don't just ask them to tell you something about them. Observe them, closely. Observe what they do and what they have done. I'm willing to bet that you will become keenly aware of the truths and the lies hidden in their actions, and aware of inconsistencies in their words that are betrayed by their behavior.

(Note: A special and posthumous "Thank you" to Dr. Milton Rokeach, whose name and work I came across while writing this essay. Dr. Rokeach held a joint appointment in the departments of Psychology and Sociology at Washington State University and was a pioneer in Values Theory, having written *The Nature of Human Values* in 1973 and *Understanding Human Values* in 1979, among others. I was fortunate to have been one of his students for several semesters in 1980 and 1981. He was a fine teacher and a good man and I always looked forward to his lectures. Dr. Rokeach passed away in 1988 at the age of 70.)

Weapons Of Social Influence

This is a reprint of my review of *Influence – The Power of Persuasion* by Robert B. Cialdini, Ph.D. It was written for and published by *Trial News* but the principles are applicable to anyone in any endeavor.

Do you want to know why you say "yes" when you would rather say "no"?

Do you want to know why you are more easily persuaded by people you like?

Would you like to have a better understanding of how and why you decide to do something, even when available contrary evidence suggests you may be better off otherwise?

Robert B. Cialdini's book *Influence – The Power of Persuasion* provides answers to these questions and more.

Cialdini's theme is this: We humans exhibit behavioral "tendencies" in many aspects of our daily lives. To a large extent these "tendencies" can fairly help to predict the responses and behaviors of people in certain situations.

We exhibit these fairly predictable behavior "tendencies" because as humans we have "capacity limitations", limitations that in this exceedingly fast-paced world of modern life lead us to the use of shortcuts. "Shortcuts" in this sense are nothing more than a retreat from time-consuming and fully informed decision-making in favor of a more primitive, automatic, "single feature" type of response.

This is not to say that shortcuts are a bad thing per se. In fact, according to the author, shortcuts are a necessary feature of our daily lives. For the most part, we tend to operate quite well on intellectual autopilot and likely would never be able to function efficiently without the ability to make shortcut decisions, filtering out the immense amount of data that is so prevalent in our lives.

But as the author points out, shortcuts can lead to vulnerability and, ultimately, exploitation if one puts too much reliance on only a single piece of relevant information.

As trial lawyers our twin objectives are to influence and to persuade, whether it be the judge, the jury, our client, the opposing attorney or even public opinion. A thorough working knowledge and understanding of the basic human behavior principles set forth in this book can give us great persuasive power and help ensure that our message has greater influence and the greater likelihood of acceptance than that of our opponents.

What follows are what Cialdini calls the "Weapons of Social Influence", seven fundamental principles that social psychologists believe govern and predictably influence human behavior. Remember, we are talking about "tendencies" of human behavior and one must keep in mind that there may be exceptions.

Weapons of Social Influence have the capacity to influence and persuade because they tend to generate "automatic" responses and trigger "predictable" behaviors. For example, social psychologists have proved experimentally that people tend to believe and be more influenced by a statement or request if the statement or request is followed by a "reason because". And this seems to hold true even if no statement of reason follows the word "because".

Another example cited by the author is the principle of "perceptual contrast", best illustrated in the context of making damages requests to judges and juries. In making damages requests, you might present the highest value damage item first, followed by the next lowest and so on. Each successive item will appear smaller by contrast (and thereby more readily acceptable) to the judge or jury.

1. **Reciprocation:** The Old Give and Take ... and Take

Cialdini's first principle of human behavior is "Reciprocation", the tendency to feel obligated to repay in kind what another has provided to us. This "triggered" feeling of indebtedness can be very powerful, obligating us even when the gift or favor is uninvited or of little value. Social psychologists have learned that once this sense of obligation has been triggered within us we may agree to make substantially larger return favors and gifts, merely to relieve ourselves from the obligation. And this appears to be so because we have become socially conditioned to feel that obligation and indebtedness produce internal discomfort and external shame, conditions to be avoided.

The companion notion of "reciprocal concession" also has practical application in the negotiation setting because we tend to feel obligated to make a concession to one who has already made a concession to us.

2 and 3. **Consistency and Commitment:** Hobgoblins of the Mind

Cialdini's second and third principles of human behavior are "Consistency" and "Commitment". The author believes that there exists a strong tendency and desire among human beings to appear consistent with what we have already done and said. Once we have taken a stand or made a choice we feel as if we must behave in accordance, even when doing so would be against our best interests.

Obtaining a commitment is the key to engaging the force and power that can bring consistency pressures to bear. Even small commitments can be used as leverage. For example, small requests and trivial commitments, once made, can produce inner changes such that the individual begins to rationalize and build a system of new justifications for having made the commitment.

The author also cites experiments tending to prove that the act of putting something in writing will lead the writer to believe in and act in a more consistent manner with that which was written and interestingly, others will also tend to believe that the writing reflects the maker's "true" attitude toward that which was written. There are a number of reasons why Cialdini believes this to be so. Most notably among them is this: written commitments require more work and more effort than verbal ones. The more effort that goes into making a commitment, the greater is its ability to influence because we tend to place a greater value on things that are attained with greater effort. Also, a written commitment is more easily made public, and the more public the stand taken, the more reluctant we tend to be to change that stand.

4. **Social Proof:** Truths – R – Us

"Social Proof" is that principle of human behavior whereby we tend to determine what is or is not correct by examining the actions of others. In other words, we assume that an action or way of thinking is more correct if others are doing or thinking it, or even if we are told that many others are doing or thinking it. This principle operates most powerfully when we are observing the behavior of people we perceive as "more like us". However, we must always be on the lookout for "pluralistic ignorance", the phenomenon sometimes known to exist when we humans place an inordinate amount of trust in the collective knowledge of the crowd, because often enough the crowd is mistaken.

5. **Liking:** The Friendly Thief

The principle of "Liking" stands for the proposition that we tend to be more psychologically compelled to influence by those we know and like. It cannot be overstated – the strength of social bonds is enormous.

Factors that reliably cause "liking", the author believes, are physical attractiveness, similarity, compliments, contact and cooperation, and conditioning and association. These characteristics, when positive, can lead to a "halo" effect whereby one positive characteristic of an individual dominates how that person is likely to be viewed by others.

Physically attractive people tend to have assigned to them such favorable traits as talent, kindness, honesty and intelligence. People we perceive as similar also tend to be more liked. Receiving a compliment and thus knowing that someone likes us is effective in producing return liking and compliance. The author also believes that we tend to be helpless in the face of praise and that we believe praise and like the provider of the praise, even when clearly false.

Lastly, we may also respond predictably to things we perceive as connected to one another. For example, we may dislike the person who brings us unpleasant information, even when the person did not cause the bad news. By contrast, positive associations occur all the time in our popular culture, through the use of celebrities for example. And interestingly, the connection need not be logical to work powerfully.

6. **Authority:** Directed Deference

The social principle of "Authority" probably arises from the deep-seated sense of obedience to authority which the author believes rests within all of us. Proof abounds of our extreme willingness to go to great lengths on the command of those we "perceive" as authoritative. And it is important to note that often the mere "appearance" of authority can be enough to trigger a sense of duty. As with all of the fundamental principles of human behavior there are, of course, real practical reasons why we can be motivated by perceived authority. For example, very early in our development we learned that obedience is right and disobedience is wrong. We learned that authority figures knew more than we did, were wiser and that they were in a position to control rewards and punishments.

"Symbols" of authority, such as titles, clothing and trappings can also lead to a kind of "automatic deference" whereby we become more susceptible to influence by the symbols themselves rather than the substance.

Of particular note here for trial lawyers is the author's discussion about experts, trustworthiness and credibility. Generally speaking, we tend to believe that authority figures (i.e. experts) know what they are talking about. And for the most part this is true, with the result that we may then relax our credibility detection mechanisms. Know this about your juries and know also that we can be much more influenced by impartial experts and by those who establish their sincerity by arguing against their own interests. Be aware, however, of the expert who seeks to establish his or her basic credibility by using this trick, arguing against his or interest on "minor issues". The bottom line, and a very important point I believe is this: there is no more credible combination, none more believable, than the demonstrated expert of proven sincerity.

7. **Scarcity:** The Rule of the Few

When the "Scarcity" principle is at work it plays on our fear of "unavailability". Things and opportunities that on their own merits hold little appeal become decidedly more attractive merely because of a pending or perceived unavailability. We humans have a tendency to place a greater value on those things that are difficult to possess and when opportunities become less available we are likely to perceive a loss of "freedom". As humans, we can become very threatened at the loss of our freedoms.

Another interesting point the author makes about the "Scarcity" principle is this: when an item is perceived to be scarce because of a demand, we then tend to value and rate that item highest of all. The bottom line is that we want an item more when it is scarce and we want it most when we are in competition for it.

One of the more interesting examples cited by the author to illustrate the "Scarcity" principle comes from research conducted by the Chicago Jury Project. The Project research team found that jurors who had been admonished to disregard certain evidence exhibited "psychological reactance" in that they tended to consider the evidence anyway, despite the admonition, and gave the evidence even greater weight. This boomerang effect is a product of what the author likens to a "commodity based" theory of persuasion.

In conclusion, the author reiterates his belief in the fundamental notion that we humans often make decisions about someone or something without first considering all of the relevant and available evidence. Rather, we take "shortcuts", using only a single, representative piece of the total available data. The tendency to take "shortcuts" can lead to mistakes but quite often the pace and stress of modern life simply demands this of us. Each of the seven principles of human behavior by themselves may provide, for the most part, usually highly reliable cues with which to govern our behavior, but this "single feature" type of decision-making can lead to automatic, mindless compliance. Clearly we need to be aware of this tendency in ourselves and in others, but as lawyers we would also be well advised to master the art of leveraging these Weapons of Social Influence on behalf of our clients.

Robert B. Cialdini, Ph.D. is an experimental social psychologist and Regents' Professor of Psychology at Arizona State University, conducting research studies and experiments in the field of psychological compliance, persuasion and change.

Flow "With" The River, Not "In" It

I learned a lesson recently, one that hurt then and hurts now. After several months of hard work on a couple of difficult cases I had the opportunity to get away to the east side of the Cascade Mountains and spend a day fishing on the Yakima River with two colleagues.

The Yakima River is one of the premier blue-ribbon trout streams in the Northwest and I've floated the stretch from Ringer to Red's or to the Roza Dam probably close to a dozen times. Sometimes I've hired a professional guide (the always friendly and easy-going Steve Joyce, proprietor of Red's Fly Shop and Resort), and other times I've borrowed a boat and made the trip with a friend. Only my good pals and colleagues have ever shared time with me on that water, and I've never had a bad day "kicking back on the mighty

Yak", even when the fish were scarce, or less than cooperative or enthusiastic for the fly I presented.

The stretch of the Yakima River that I like to fish rests at the bottom of a gentle canyon, and it's scenic, to be sure. It's also officially classified as "desert" and it rarely rains in the Yakima River Canyon, even in otherwise rain-soaked Washington. You can see bighorn sheep, deer, bald eagles and beaver, to name just some of the local wildlife.

The Yakima River stretch that we set out to fish that day is an easy two-hour drive from Seattle ... just right for a good cup of coffee and some early morning conversation. When we arrived at the designated launch site I noticed it was a few degrees cooler than I'd been used to. Normally I fish the Yak in the heat of summer, when the flows are high and fast, the days are long and the crickets are in song. Good summer fishing on the Yakima means presenting floating grasshopper and other terrestrial insect imitations up tight to the shoreline, mending the line and achieving a natural "dead drift".

But on this day, September 23, the river flows were lower, and the most productive fishing was to be had by casting sub-surface aquatic insect imitations known as "nymphs". I have less experience "nymphing" than surface-fly fishing, and I probably felt a bit uncertain about that. For whatever reason, I was feeling anxious. Certainly the cooler temperatures and the fact that some atypical rain fell on us contributed to my uneasiness. It didn't help that for the first time ever I left most of my warm clothes behind in the car. But relaxation be damned, I was there to fish and catch fish, so I worked and worked and worked at it, casting time after time, mending my line, working the drifts, and untangling more than a few knots. I caught a few fish. But I wasn't relaxing. If anything, I was trying harder than I needed to. I certainly was not flowing with the river.

My colleague companions seemed to be having a good time though, and to be sure, we all had our laughs along the way, as well as a sip or two of a fine spirit from Kentucky that helped keep the chill away and came in handy for a celebratory toast when one or another of us caught, or lost a fish.

In the heat of July and August, it's not unusual to fish the Yakima River until 8:00 in the evening or later, but with the shorter days of late-September upon us a boat full of fishermen needs to be mindful of the time. By 5:00 p.m. we were still an hour or more from the take-out site and we decided it would be best to spend more time rowing and less time fishing … at least that's what my colleagues decided. I wanted to keep fishing and, by God, I did just that. I stood up in the back of that drift boat where I'd been fishing all morning and afternoon and refused to call it a day. On a couple of occasions our boat hit rocks and I'd nearly get thrown back into my seat, or worse, but I don't like casting from a sitting position when I'm on the river, so stand I did; not the smartest thing in the world, but a calculated risk. I was, after all, there to catch fish, right?

Finally, toward 7:00 p.m. we came up to a vantage where we could see the take-out spot. My colleague who was rowing the boat eased us toward the bank and we slowly floated along toward the take-out in about a foot-and-a-half of water. I still hadn't given up the fishing and was casting away, hoping for just one more catch… one more shred of evidence that would prove, to myself and others, just what a good fisherman I am.

Then it happened. A sound heard – grinding; a jolt felt – the boat no longer drifting but, instead, stopped and stopped hard; surprise felt – I'm tumbling. It all seemed to happen very fast, but I know that my body went over in a kind of awkward slow motion… lower limbs still in the boat while the upper parts were beginning to feel the cold water, the swift current and the hard rocks. My left hand landed on a big smooth rock and for a moment I steadied, then the boat caught the current once again and as it resumed its trajectory down-river I stayed put… in the river.

My waders instantly filled with the cold water. I knew I wasn't in danger, it was too shallow and too close to shore. But I was very wet and I was cold. I also knew, almost immediately after I righted myself and stood back up, that my fly rod and reel had tumbled in with me. I looked in the water and saw nothing but the rocky bottom. My companions, still in the boat, had floated by this time 100 or so feet downstream. I don't think they saw the equipment in my hand tumble in with me. I immediately started looking, dazed and a bit frantic… and walking, as best one can in a swift current on slippery rocks, downstream. I couldn't or didn't see where it went. It was dusk and getting darker, making visibility more difficult by the minute. I knew that seconds, literally, mattered and as each second passed I knew it was less and less likely I'd ever find that Lefty Kreh signature, Temple Fork Outfitters, four-piece, five-weight fly rod with the Ross Rhythm reel I'd bought just three years earlier. I never did find it, even with the help of my friends. It was just too dark, I was too wet, and it was too late; we had to get the boat on the trailer and drive home.

I turned attention to myself and conducted an inventory. My waders have a chest pocket. I opened the pocket and it was, like the rest of my wading outfit, full of water. Inside the pocket, in a puddle of water, was my almost-new cell phone. Nearly everyone who has a cell phone has heard stories of phones that made unscheduled trips in the laundry machine, the toilet bowl, a paint can… the list goes on. Long story short… the phone drowned. As one good friend said "Dave, you destroyed your Droid". Later he added insult to injury, saying I had a "drowned Droid".

Yes, in the space of a couple of seconds I had lost some fine (and expensive) fishing equipment, had ruined a cell phone, had bruised my hand, had gotten soaked, and had a good day pretty much spoiled. It's one thing to fall in the water and let the other guys have a laugh at your expense. It's quite another to have a casualty loss, on top of a $50 gas bill and a $32 shuttle fee. Day on the river with your friends… priceless; full price for the day… close to a thousand dollars, give or take a hundred; total number of fish I caught… four or five; average price per pound of those fish (we catch and release 'em)… I don't even want to think about it.

Well, I've learned and earned enough perspective in the last 32 months to know that this wasn't a life and death matter, or anywhere close to one, and in the grand scheme of things, really didn't amount to a hill of beans in this crazy world. But it wasn't long after we secured the boat on the trailer that I realized I had a problem… and a lesson learned… and that lesson was this: I've got to learn to relax and have some fun. This was a day that was supposed to be all about fun, and all about relaxing. But the actual events of the day proved that I hadn't really had fun or relaxed because I was too competitive, whether with myself or my buddies, or too wrapped up in an ego-driven macho show of "Who's the better fisherman?" to really let go and enjoy myself. It's because of that ego-driven behavior, and my inability or unwillingness to relax and just "be", to just "flow with the river" that I believe caused me to lose awareness of the potential for a tumble, spill and loss like the one I experienced.

It's been a tough ten days since then. I've felt bad, sad, mad and anxious, really anxious. I'm upset that something as stupid as my own competitive nature (or is it insecurity) led me to be so careless. I'm upset at the loss of a quality rod and reel that I valued and that, though easily replaceable, are only replaceable at a dear price. And I'm upset that I had my cell phone with me on the river. To my credit, I didn't answer calls when the phone rang, but I would look to see who the caller was, and I did check my emails, for goodness sake … on the river … on a mid-week fishing getaway.

So that's the story and that's the lesson; one I've learned before, unfortunately. Looking back, it wouldn't have mattered how many fish I caught that day considering the way it ended. All I know is that it was preventable, and the keys to preventability, in that situation, I believe, were to slow down, take more than a couple of deep breaths, take full advantage of the opportunities to feel and be grateful for the place and time on Earth at that moment, slow down, don't rush, sit down, sit back, let go of the critical ego-self, and enjoy the journey.

Since then I've had friends point out a couple of silver linings, one of those being that when I finally can afford it I can buy a new outfit that's even better (and even more expensive) than the one I lost; the other being that some months earlier I managed to hook and land a really beautiful fish with that same outfit and I have a picture that captures the memory framed and hanging on my office wall. I look at it every day. It's a steady reminder of things gained, things lost, things that cost, and my hard-earned lesson learned in those last competitive and frenetic minutes on the Yak.

Life By A Thousand Cuts

Today is November 26, 2010, one year from the day that I started this project. In that time, I've written 26 essays (26 short of the number I set out to write). It's been therapeutic, writing these essays, and a privilege to receive your feedback. I learned a lot about myself, whether looking back, examining the present or looking forward to whatever the future might bring, and I learned a little bit about others who read the posts and took the time to write thoughtful and much-appreciated comments. You probably noticed that I didn't reply to the comments and that was by design. Every essay provided the opportunity to say what I wanted or needed to say at the time, and it seemed more honoring of each of you to let your thoughts and words of reply stand on their own.

It's been an interesting year, with, as usual, plenty of mistakes and achievements of good things too. I nearly made my goal of avoiding the hospital all-together (save for one late-summer visit to the ER that probably could have been avoided, but surely didn't seem avoidable at the time, and save for several trips to hospitals to visit others in my life that I care about). No matter the point of view, looking in or looking out, I can't escape that I find hospitals to be interesting places full of interesting people. Where else are all the processes of life and death so immediately on display and where else can we be so attuned to the suffering of a person in one room and so detached from that of persons in other rooms nearby?

I'm constantly amazed at how the cards of life turn over, one-by-one and day-by-day. Surprising things happened that I never would have imagined this time a year ago. That's the way things are though ... lots of day-to-day sameness with occasional moments of love, laughter, luck (good and bad), pain, grief, fear, anxiousness, gain and loss. I call it "life by a thousand cuts" because in looking back over this year, and these essays, I'm aware of a trend, and the trend is that there seem to be more stories of hard lessons learned than the other way around. Certainly the hard lessons are as much if not more a part of the fabric of my life as the easy ones and when they cut are often painful, to varying degrees.

When I was twelve or thirteen years old I would listen to the "Woodstock" triple album. The liner notes written by the album's producer Eric Blackstead address the technical flaws heard in the recordings ... the scratches, pops, hiss and editing miscues that came with the challenges of the live recording process. Blackstead urges the listener to think of these flaws as "like scars in fine leather". Well, since none of us escapes life without at least a few scars, I'm going to let Blackstead's words be a reminder to keep a positive mental attitude and accept, maybe even embrace, the scars from life's inevitable thousand cuts.

Finally, for no reason other than I want to say it I continue to be grateful for the privilege of each and every day and each and every encounter. I believe no life is very meaningful unless shared meaningfully and I thank all of the good and interesting people who have been a part of sharing my world this year. You make it a better place.

Afterword

In the four years since the essays (and one very short story) that make up this book were written there have been many more "cuts", both of flesh and in the fabric of my life. I've learned these cuts of life are easier to embrace once they are viewed from the perspective of the rear-view mirror and less so when they are happening in the moment. But these cuts of life are gifts and they continue to remind me of the great privilege it is to have this life and live it fully to the extent that nature and the fates will allow. Pain of any kind is a signal that something needs to be changed and change is not always easy, no matter whether it comes about by force or conscious choice. The cuts of my life have often been painful but they have led me to where I am today and where I am today, as I write these words, seems to me a pretty good place.

The brightest reminder of that, daily, is the fact that I am now six years a "survivor". I made it past the clinical benchmark "five year survival" period with no recurrence of the cancer that threw my life into a sudden and unexpected panic. Survival was by no means a guarantee and later, in 2013, when the fact of being cure was all but assured, I listened as my oncologist related to an assemblage of my peers that my "number" had been fifty, as in a fifty percent chance that I would have survived five years with no recurrence of the cancer that had been diagnosed, surgically removed, doused with chemotherapy, bombarded by radiation and left me with residuals I'd rather not go into the details of here. Early in the game he had told me the number was sixty-five percent. I found ways, anxiously, to live with that. Ten deep breaths can keep anxiety at bay. Journaling is helpful. And I could tell myself "Well, at least the odds are in my favor". Had I known then that the picture changed to nothing more than a mere coin flip I would certainly have experienced more worry and anxiety than is comfortable to ponder even today, successfully "cured" and far removed in time from those events.

I'd like to share an interesting story that resonates with me and the themes of this book as I see them. In the late-summer of 2011, after settling into the hope and expectation of what was looking like a successful recovery from cancer I began, suddenly, experiencing symptoms that were cause for alarm (copious bleeding, intense pain and discomfort, and no sign of improvement will sound the alarms every time). I paid an unscheduled visit to my oncologist. He, in turn, ordered a CT scan. Not liking what he saw on the CT scan he had me pay a visit to my surgeon. My surgeon was not enthusiastic and more than hinted at what I was not ready to hear, that it looked like the cancer had not only returned but returned with a vengeance. Complicating matters, I was to leave for a week-long vacation the next day. My surgeon recommended I take the vacation anyway and I did. It was a terrible week. I continued to have the uncomfortable and distracting symptoms, got served with a hugely important and poorly-timed work matter that required much of my time, energies and attention, and overall worried whether I would have the emotional resources to go on, fighting another battle that I sensed would be, statistically, a losing one.

After the vacation I saw my oncologist again. He suggested a PET CT. A PET CT is an exquisite diagnostic imaging device. In my one and only previous experience with it nearly four years earlier the PET CT had confirmed the fact, existence and location of cancer. The technician, a delightful and comforting individual, first administered the nuclear medicine intravenously. The medicine is designed to highlight, visually, areas of rapid cellular growth as measured by consumption of sugars. Besides being immortal, cancer cells can grow fast and they are hungry. As I understand, the diagnostic scale runs from zero to ten, with ten being very bright on the film image and very bad. Several days later I returned to my oncologist's office. He told me – and showed me – the imaging film and said the PET CT number was seven or eight on the brightness scale and that, above the number four on the scale, "All bets are off". I asked him what did he think was my new "number" (my five year survival chance) now? He replied that such things weren't really a matter of discussion at that time. He did say that we ought to have a CT-guided "punch-needle" biopsy for additional confirmation before doing anything further.

If you're squeamish about needles then you probably wouldn't care to see the one they used to take samples from deep in my rectum. While I don't know exactly how long that prober of a needle was, I'm making the educated guess that it had to be eight or nine inches, maybe longer. But I didn't feel a thing thanks to the predictably sedating effects of anesthesia, expertly and as I recall, compassionately delivered.

I waited anxiously during those several days while the three tissue samples were biopsied at some distant and probably windowless lab and then I paid yet another visit to my surgeon for the results. It had been nearly a month since this un-forecast tornado touched down and in that time there had been little cause for hope, really, except that I kept holding on, in the back of my mind, to the fact that throughout the recovery period thus far my CEA level (CEA stands for carcinoembryonic antigen and the CEA level is a measure of the amount of a certain protein that may appear in the blood of some people who have certain kinds of cancers, especially cancer of the large intestine, colon and rectum) had been consistently normal, and also to the fact that on several occasions in the previous three years my surgeon had sunk his deft hands and instruments in my belly, colon and rectum and each time digging around in there had taken samples and the samples had always tested negative. I recall waiting, as it always seems to be, an interminably long, uncertain and lonely time in the examining room. I recall everything about it. The metal lamp and bright light; the magazines; the exam table, with its paper sheet that I had lay on during earlier visits when the surgical drains were removed and when the stitches had been taken out and while being probed in undignified manner; the tile floor.

Finally he, the surgeon, walked in. I didn't want to hear it, a death sentence or, at best, the hope, if it can be called that, of another long uncertain battle that would further diminish already weakened flesh and spirit and keep me longer, perhaps ever, from achieving the things I needed and still wanted to do. But here was the news: the biopsies were… negative! To the genuine surprise – a better word might be amazement – of the medical establishment that was charged with my care at the time, and with ninety-five percent accuracy (as close to a sure thing as there is in medicine) the cells in the specimen tissues contained no evidence of cancer. I would be spared this horrible fate. And here's where it got interesting, to me at least, as I look back on the experience. I floated out of that office. I felt a new perspective from the gift of that new lease on life. A tremendous weight had lifted. I became a new person. In that moment and in the moments, hours, days, weeks and years after I continue to remind myself how grateful I felt for that reprieve and how grateful I am for what I have and for the opportunity to be here. Whenever I am asked "How are things?" or "How are you doing?" I invariably reply "I'm just grateful to be here". And that's the absolute genuine, congruent truth.

That mantra of gratefulness is a gift, neatly wrapped and available to anyone willing to open it; at least that's my opinion. Bill Bryson, in his exceptional *A Short History of Nearly Everything*, writes about the nearly impossible fact of our existence as a species on this or any planet and the luck upon random luck that allows us, we people, and ourselves, to be here. He says: "Consider the fact that for 3.8 billion years, a period of time older than the Earth's mountains and rivers and oceans, every one of your forebears on both sides has been attractive enough to find a mate, healthy enough to reproduce, and sufficiently blessed by fate and circumstances to live long enough to do so. Not one of your pertinent ancestors was squashed, devoured, drowned, starved, stranded, stuck fast, untimely wounded, or otherwise deflected from its life's quest of delivering a tiny charge of genetic material to the right partner at the right moment in order to perpetuate the only possible sequence of hereditary combinations that could result – eventually, astoundingly, and all too briefly – in you." He emphasizes the point again: "… for nearly four billion years our ancestors have managed to slip through a series of closing doors every time we needed them to." Finally, Bryson reminds us that not only are we lucky (doubly lucky, triply lucky … I say *infinitely lucky*) to be here and to have the privilege of existence, but we also seem to be gifted with the capacity, beyond any of Earth's other inhabitants, to appreciate it. And as if that isn't enough, we also have the ability, should we wish, to make it better.

So as I write this at fifty-five, nearly fifty-six years now on this planet, I want to share what I have learned, that life is short and for some, sadly, even shorter. But to me there's no denying the privilege of a life of any duration. We have only the one chance to experience our individual lives. I am grateful for it and I recommend the prescription "Just be grateful to be here" to everyone. It's not overly dramatic and it's neither religion nor cult nor illusion nor magic. It's simply a recognition that each of us has been gifted, almost impossibly, with something beyond extraordinary, a life, this one life, and the time, ways and means to appreciate it.